TEACHER SUBJECT IDE
PROFESSIONAL PRACTICE

Teacher Subject Identity in Professional Practice focuses on a key, but neglected, element of a teacher's identity: that of their subject expertise. Studies of teachers' professional practice have shown the importance of a teacher's identity and the extent to which it can affect their resilience, commitment and ultimately their effectiveness.

Drawing upon narrative research undertaken with a range of teachers over a period of 14 years, the book explores how subject expertise can play a significant role in teacher identity, acting as a professional compass guiding teachers at all levels of their professional practice. It reveals powerful individual stories of meaning-making which highlight the dynamic importance of teachers' subject expertise.

The book's metaphor of a professional compass goes to the heart of teacher professionalism and provides a valuable mechanism to enable teachers to respond to challenges they face in their daily practice. It enables teachers to consider the moral dimensions of their practice and can constitute a significant component in professional formation and identity. Throughout the book the importance of subject expertise for teachers' professional practice is explored at a range of scales, from the classroom to broad education policy, and at different stages of a teacher's career, which offers readers a deeper understanding of the importance of subject expertise for teachers.

Teacher Subject Identity in Professional Practice makes a significant contribution to an under-researched area. It identifies the role and significance of teachers' subject expertise as a dimension of their teacher identity. The book is key reading for teacher educators, policy makers and researchers with an interest in teachers' professional development and practice.

Clare Brooks is the Head of Curriculum, Pedagogy and Assessment and Senior Lecturer in Geography Education at UCL Institute of Education, UK.

Foundations and Futures of Education

Peter Aggleton UNSW, Australia
Sally Power Cardiff University, UK
Michael Reiss Institute of Education, University of London, UK

Foundations and Futures of Education focuses on key emerging issues in education as well as continuing debates within the field. The series is inter-disciplinary, and includes historical, philosophical, sociological, psychological and comparative perspectives on three major themes: the purposes and nature of education; increasing interdisciplinarity within the subject; and the theory-practice divide.

Previous titles include:

TEACHER SUBJECT IDENTITY IN PROFESSIONAL PRACTICE

Teaching with a professional compass

Clare Brooks

Routledge
Taylor & Francis Group

LONDON AND NEW YORK

First published 2016
by Routledge
2 Park Square, Milton Park, Abingdon, Oxon OX14 4RN

and by Routledge
711 Third Avenue, New York, NY 10017

Routledge is an imprint of the Taylor & Francis Group, an informa business

British Library Cataloguing in Publication Data
A catalogue record for this book is available from the British Library

Library of Congress Cataloging in Publication Data
A catalog record for this book has been requested

ISBN: 978-1-138-02590-5 (hbk)
ISBN: 978-1-138-02591-2 (pbk)
ISBN: 978-1-315-77477-0 (ebk)

Typeset in Bembo
by Swales & Willis Ltd, Exeter, Devon, UK
Printed in Great Britain by Ashford Colour Press Ltd

CONTENTS

FIGURES

TABLES

ACKNOWLEDGEMENTS

This research would not have been possible without the kindness, generosity and openness of all the teachers that have supported me and taken part in my research over the years. Particular thanks go to the teachers who agreed to take part early on, thinking this was part of my PhD and not realizing that our continued relationship would last this long. My sincere thanks to you. I would also like to acknowledge with thanks the schools and colleges where they worked, and the colleagues that were also happy to talk to me. I am also incredibly grateful to my colleagues in the geography education community who have helped me to refine and develop my ideas and who have been generous enough to offer critical feedback and commentary along the way. I am also indebted to the Series Editors for their careful consideration, words of encouragement and supportive feedback which have all helped to improve this work significantly.

On a more personal note, my thanks go to Martin. Without his emotional and practical support this would still be just an idea.

Acknowledgement is given to the Geographical Association for the publication of Figure 3.1, Ideological traditions and geography, from Rawling, E.M. (2001: 32) and for the publication of the curriculum making diagram from www.geography.org.uk/cpdevents/curriculum/curriculummaking.

Acknowledgement is also given to Taylor & Francis for the publication of Figure 4.1, A framework for history teachers' knowledge, from Husbands, C. (2011: 93).

1

BEING A TEACHER IN THIS DAY AND AGE

Steven had always wanted to be a geography teacher. It was the reason he studied geography at school, and at university. On his degree course, Steven was one of the few people who were clear about what they wanted to do after graduation. His focus on becoming a geography teacher influenced the module choices he made at university: unlike many of his friends, he chose not to specialize in physical or human geography, but to maintain a balance between both.

> Having no particular specialism was deliberate, to gain a balance, but additionally because my genuine interest was evident in all chosen areas of focus . . . I feel Geography is a wonderful vehicle to explore not only processes, features, concepts and events but also additionally people's values and attitudes.

Steven wanted to build his knowledge in all areas of the discipline, even if it meant studying aspects of geography he found less engaging. For Steven, balance was what made geography distinctive from other disciplines. Too much emphasis on one side or the other, he felt was 'out of balance', and could prevent people from making informed decisions.

> I worked for a mining company in Scotland which, from a teaching point of view, was an interesting context because you got to see why people think what they do – getting to see the other side of the argument. It's far too easy to give the view of the conservationists: the environmentalists' viewpoint. It's quite an easy one that kids empathize with, but I think it needs to be a balanced argument and having that experience has exposed me to that.

After teaching geography for ten years, balance continued to be important to Steven, influencing how he viewed his students.

> One of the things that I believe in as a teacher and not just as a geography teacher is that a kid comes into the classroom with a lot of baggage and you can't just teach that person as a separate entity without the baggage – you've got to take into consideration the baggage.

Steven thought that geography would be useful to his students because it would enable them to function in many aspects of their lives.

> I would hope that they would leave having enjoyed the subject, even if it's not their passion, appreciating that it can be someone else's passion. I would hope that they would leave with a desire to still find out more, with an ability to find out how something else works, or to appreciate why people reacted in a certain way to an event, to appreciate the fact that an issue isn't purely black and white, that there are several issues to the story. There are several reasons for why things can happen and I would hope that they would try to offer an explanation to an awful lot of things that crop up. If they have a passion for geography or to find out more about it, that's the ultimate job.

Fifteen years later, Steven was no longer teaching geography. He had moved to Scotland, and was working in a school as a support teacher. He decided to move to Scotland when his last public examination class came to the end of their studies, and he decided that he had had enough of teaching in England. He described how the changes that were happening in his school had been having an impact on his practice: the increasing pressures of accountability were taking him away from doing what he considered to be a 'good job'. Steven decided to move to Scotland where he could be the sort of teacher he wanted to be, even if that meant losing some of what he described as the 'professional status' he had built up.

Steven's story is not unusual. There is a teaching recruitment and retention crisis, particularly in England where four out of ten teachers leave the profession within their first year (*The Telegraph* 2015). In the US, many teachers are approaching retirement age and there are not enough new entrants to the profession to fill the gap. The OECD report (2005) on the international picture of teacher recruitment and retention offers the following summary:

> Although the information is often patchy a broad picture of concerns across countries has emerged about:
>
> - 'qualitative' shortfalls: whether enough teachers have the knowledge and skills to meet school needs;
> - limited connections between teacher education, teachers' professional development, and school needs;
> - maintaining an adequate supply of good quality teachers, especially in high demand subject areas;
> - the image and status of teaching: teachers often feel that their work is undervalued;

- long term trends in the composition of the teaching workforce, e.g. fewer 'high achievers' and males;
- sometimes high rates of teacher attrition, especially among new teachers;
- the impact of high workloads, stress and poor working environments on job satisfaction and teaching effectiveness;
- limited means in most countries to recognise and reward teachers' work;
- in some countries, a large over-supply of qualified teachers, which raises its own policy challenges;
- inequitable distribution of teachers among schools, and concerns over whether students in disadvantaged areas have the quality teachers that they need.

(OECD 2005: 5)

As the report highlights, one area of concern is the changing nature of teaching and the effect it can have on teacher effectiveness. For example, the National Union of Teachers (Galton and MacBeath 2008) highlights the 'intensification' of teachers' work across England (as well as in Canada, Hong Kong, New Zealand and Australia), stating: '"Intensification" is a prevailing concern, leaving many teachers with the feeling that time-consuming initiatives are designed to control performance rather than benefit pupils' educational development' (Galton and MacBeath 2008: 2). The report relates these findings to the high incidence of teacher burnout and concludes that managerial workforce remodelling style reforms fail to get to the heart of teachers' concerns.

The deprofessionalizing effect of accountability reforms has been widely recognized (see Whitty 2008). Research into the impact of the Standards Agenda in England (Day 2004) emphasizes how education policy can affect the work of individual schools, which ultimately presents dilemmas for individual teachers. Day (2012) outlines how much of the research into the impact of these reforms has taken a rather negative view of the effect they can have on teachers, and has neglected to explore the experiences of teachers who have flourished and who continue to work effectively within the same reform context. This is echoed in the call for teachers to be more resilient in their work (see Sammons *et al.* 2007).

Indeed, the idea that teachers should be more resilient in the light of education reforms has led some to question the nature of teacher recruitment. The OECD (2005) has acknowledged that the recruitment of quality teachers is a concern for both high performing and developing economies. The concern is to ensure that appropriately qualified teachers are recruited who have the qualities that will enable them to stay in the profession long term. But these concerns are focused on teachers themselves rather than the rapidly changing contexts that teachers find themselves in. In turn, these changing contexts show remarkable similarities around the globe (Ball 2012). Day and Gu (2010) suggest that these reforms share similar characteristics. They:

- are happening because governments believe that by intervening to change the conditions under which students learn, they can accelerate improvements, raise standards of achievement and somehow increase economic competitiveness;

- address implicit worries of governments concerning a perceived fragmentation of personal and social values in society;
- result in an increased workload for teachers;
- do not pay attention to teachers' identities – arguably central to motivation, efficacy, commitment, job satisfaction and wellbeing;
- emanate from a deficit view of teachers; and
- do not acknowledge the importance of teacher wellbeing and commitment.

(Day and Gu 2010: 25)

Day and Gu call for a refocus on teacher identity as a response to the pressures of reform, arguing that it is key to understanding teacher effectiveness.

Teacher identity is indeed central to understanding how teachers adapt to reform. Whilst leaving teaching might seem out-of-step for someone like Steven who had always wanted to be a teacher, working in a support capacity is entirely in line with what he values – balance. Balance is one of the factors which drew him to teaching geography in the first place and it continues as a major theme in his professional life. A desire to achieve balance in his own life is reflected in his reasons for moving to a rural part of Scotland, in his personal interest in the environment and environmental stewardship, in his concern that schools look after their students, and in his views on what young people should be learning in schools.

In my discussions with Steven, he traced where this emphasis on balance had come from and why it was so important to him. It began at school when he felt drawn to school geography as the only subject which helped him to understand and explain both the natural and the social forces that shape the world. It went on to influence his university module choices, and it has informed his practice as a geography teacher. Steven describes how balance is needed to understand the world and to function effectively within it. For him, balance is a word that is profoundly geographical, as it reflects the disciplinary concerns of both physical and human geography, and how they come together to make up the unified discipline (see Matthews and Herbert 2004). For him, the idea of balance is also moral as it mediates against extremism and represents fairness.

Steven's story, which was told to me over a period of 15 years, is remarkable for its consistency and coherence. This suggests that these values are a sustaining feature of his professional practice, and can be seen as an aspect of his identity. What is interesting to note is that the idea stems from the subject he teaches. For Stephen, balance is a geographical idea which appears to act like a professional compass, guiding his professional practice. He uses this compass to navigate the professional landscapes he has found himself in.

Professional knowledge landscapes

To understand Steven's story, and in particular why he chose to move away from teaching geography, it is useful to consider the contexts of his professional practice or, in other words, his professional knowledge landscapes.

The idea that teachers work within a professional knowledge landscape was first introduced by Clandinin and Connelly (1995). They describe these landscapes as being made up of 'sacred stories' which come from official discourses, and which may be in conflict with teachers' own stories of their professional practice. Clandinin and Connelly argue that this creates dilemmas which are knowledge dilemmas as they represent a conflict between official knowledge, as represented by policies or directives from their school or official discourses, and the personal knowledge of the teacher. In this book I want to go a stage further and suggest that these landscapes can play a profound role in affecting how teachers work and can, in effect, 'make teachers up', in that they can influence not just what teachers do but also who they are.

One of the ways that teachers can respond to such sacred stories is to draw upon dimensions of their professional identity which reflect their values about education and teaching. The argument that I am presenting here is that these values can be traced back to a teacher's subject identity. In other words, teacher subject identity can be an important driver in how teachers respond to reforms in education.

Whilst the narratives Clandinin and Connelly describe are vivid accounts, their focus is on localized and individual experiences of education contexts. More recent work has highlighted the pervasiveness of neoliberal education policies on how schools operate (Ball, Maguire and Braun 2012) and on individual teachers' work (Day et al. 2007). What is missing from all these accounts is what qualities teachers need to operate effectively in these contexts and how they can develop these qualities.

The importance of teacher identity

Stories like Steven's are important. Large scale surveys like the VITAE project reveal general patterns and trends in teachers' working lives (Day et al. 2007; Sammons et al. 2007; Day and Gu 2010). However, to make full use of their findings, we need to understand more about how teachers make sense of their working lives. The VITAE project set out to explore the impact of the Standards Agenda on teachers in England. The report makes two valuable and important assertions: that teachers' commitment can have a positive impact on students' attainment and that effective teachers require resilience in order to sustain that commitment. The research focuses specifically on teachers' professional and personal lives and charts the complexity of how motivation and commitment can ebb and flow through the duration of a career. However, the research does not pin down where teacher identity or commitment come from. It leaves unanswered the questions:

- Why are some teachers more committed than others?
- What influences teachers' resilience?
- What can we do to promote these qualities in future teachers?

Whilst the research that underpins this book did not set out to answer these questions, the findings, narratives and stories that I present here throw some light on these issues. In talking to teachers over a period of some years (varying between four and fifteen) about their personal and professional lives, significant themes are evident about teacher identity and how identity relates to professional practice. Conducting this research over time can also reveal how changes in contexts can influence and affect these identities. Teacher identity is not static but can change and can be context sensitive. To understand teachers we need to understand the contexts they work in.

Clandinin and Connelly (1995) are right to acknowledge that professional knowledge landscapes have both a knowledge and a moral dimension. But research in this area has yet to explore the school subject and academic disciplinary contribution to the professional knowledge landscape. Indeed, the recent research on neoliberal education policies and their impact on schools (Maguire *et al.* 2011; Kaniuka 2012; Hatch 2013) presents a challenge to subject-based expertise. These policies can, on one hand, focus on the importance of (subject) knowledge as the basis for teachers' authority, but on the other represent the teaching profession as one predicated on technical skill and lacking any specific knowledge-based component. Teachers can be left wondering what role their subject knowledge can play in their professional practice.

The implicit values and beliefs expressed in the professional knowledge landscape communicate clear expectations about practice. The official or sacred stories can influence the work of teachers, and can be observed at the level of classroom practice (as outlined by Clandinin and Connelly 1995), and at the level of the school (note the title of Ball, Maguire and Braun's 2012 book *How Schools Do Policy*). These stories can exhibit both values and beliefs and also expectations about practice. To behave in a way that is counter to these stories can be extremely challenging for teachers. These challenges can be revealed in the narratives or stories that teachers tell about their work. By understanding these contexts in this way, we can deepen our understanding of how and why some teachers appear to flourish in some contexts that others find dysfunctional and why some teachers leave the profession and some teachers stay (as explored in Chapter Two).

Professional practice

The aim of the research discussed in this book is to understand the importance of teacher subject identity. The focus is on the experience of individual teachers and how they make sense of their work, and in particular how this sense-making can influence their practice.

The research takes a broad view of teachers' professional practice. The classroom is the main site of teachers' work, and is the key location for their interactions with students and colleagues. But professional practice can also recognize that some of teachers' work takes place outside the classroom. The view of activist professionalism as outlined by Sachs (2003) recognizes that teachers may also be active in their subject communities and their school communities, and within other networks. Teachers may have perspectives on school policies, education policies, and research from both education and subject fields that can also influence their practice. Being a professional may spill over into their personal lives. This book therefore takes a broad view of professional practice as encompassing the work of teachers in and beyond the classroom. This view of professionalism is that of a dynamic idea of 'being a teacher', a process that is being constantly made and remade in every-day actions and interactions. This perspective is summed up in Barnett's (2008) description of 'being a professional', drawing upon Heidegger's notion of being. This is not a static notion of being, suggestive of a state of arrival, but a dynamic sense of continual engagement and striving towards, as described by Barnett:

> Being is not just how individuals are in the world, but also how they stand in time, backwards and forwards. Therefore "being" has possibilities and is always restlessly searching, working forwards, even if it knows not where or to what.
>
> *(Barnett 2008: 193)*

How then can this professional practice best be explored? To reflect the focus on individual teachers and how they understand their work and subject identity, the method applied in this work was designed so that teachers were able to articulate their own perspectives about their work. In this research, I adopted a narrative methodology to enable them to do just that.

Narrative

Narrative is an established feature of research into teachers' professional lives and practice. Goodson *et al.* (2011) argue that we live in an age of narratives, where media and politicians regularly use narratives to define messages and to persuade others, and that narratives have become ubiquitous in how we make sense of our lives. Within the field of teacher education, Parker *et al.* (2011: 5) note how such an approach can be useful in highlighting the complexity of understanding educa-tion by 'grounding our teacher education practices in experience'. The value of this approach is that it gives 'voice' to individual teachers in recounting not just their experiences, but how they make sense of those experiences. Narrative has become a popular methodology to understand teachers' professional practice and identity.

Narrative approaches can emphasize the individual nature of how teachers respond to changing contexts and influences, highlighting the distinctions in atti-tude, performance and strategies they use (Ball and Goodson 1985). Elbaz (1990) argues that 'The accomplishment of story thus always involves both the creation of a coherent meaning and the successful resolution of whatever conflict threatens meaning' (Elbaz 1990: 38). Therefore, when we look at teachers' narratives or sto-ries, it is important to recognize that the narrative is not necessarily a recollection of actual events, but can represent the individual's meaning-making as he or she generates a narrative to explain and justify his or her actions. This is particularly true of a research situation, where a participant is generating a narrative for the purpose of explaining something to the interviewer. Under these circumstances, narratives are constructed to show justification not causality (Goodson *et al.* 2011). Indeed the process of constructing a narrative can be a learning experience in itself (ibid.).

This distinction between what we can learn from narratives and their episte-mological value is important in relation to the claims made in this book. Goodson and Sikes (2001) argue that, by scrutinizing storylines, we can begin to understand how people are responding to changing historical and cultural circumstances. To understand this significance, it is important to link narratives with identity, learning and agency. In this research, teachers were asked to discuss their practice, their professional contexts and how they rationalize influences on their practice. The research is descriptive rather than normative: so the focus has been on finding out how teachers make sense of their work, rather than how they should or could do so. But this does not mean that the accounts are taken as factual recall, as the stories told inevitably feature elements of justification. Life narratives are constructed in order to make clear why it was thought necessary − morally, socially, psychologically (rather than causally) − for life to have gone in a particular way (Bruner 1990). Therefore narratives are not just about what has happened but how the individual has made sense of what has happened, and how they use that understanding to make meaning.

MacLure takes this a step further and sees narrative use within identity research as a form of argument which is 'inescapably moral: identity claims are inevitably bound up with justifications of conduct and belief' (1993: 320). Understanding narrative as argument emphasizes the difference between narratives and factual recall: narratives are social constructions that people use to make sense of themselves. However, to understand these narratives, it is important to take them seriously on their own terms and 'not just as the expression of something underlying or overarching' (Goodson *et al.* 2011: 127; see also Biesta 2010). This methodological approach to the research is in line with its emphasis on finding out why individual teachers behave in the way they do. The act of teaching can be driven by a range of values, brought together and made meaningful by the teacher. Teaching has a clear set of professional ethics (see Lunt 2008) and academic disciplines are themselves values-driven (as described in Chapter Three). This is a moral landscape of practice, an exploration of which can help to understand how teachers behave in the way they do.

Teacher identity

The aim of this work then is to understand stories like the one told by Steven: to understand how teachers react to their local contexts through an analysis of what drives their work. The emphasis is on understanding the interplay between context and identity, and in particular the role of subject identity as a driving influence of professional practice. Previous research into teacher professional identity has neglected to explore the role that subject identity can play.

Having worked in initial teacher education for over ten years, I have interviewed a large number of prospective teachers, many of whom profess that their desire to enter teaching is largely driven by a love of, and desire to continue working with, their subject specialism. Such anecdotal observations have been made by others (Morgan and Lambert 2005; Turvey 2005). However, research on teacher professional identity rates subject identity as a benign influence with only nine per cent of teachers suggesting that they initially chose teaching as a career because they wanted to teach their subject (Day *et al.* 2007: 222).

It is my contention that, for many subject specialists (and I certainly do not suggest that this is the case for all teachers), subject identity is such a strong part of their own personal and professional identity that it becomes tacit, implicit and difficult to articulate. It may well be the case that teachers have not identified the subject as being a key influence on their teaching careers because it is so much a part of who they are. All the more reason then to focus on subject identity and how it can influence practice.

Subject knowledge and subject identity

Subject identity, the term used in this work, is not to be confused with subject knowledge. This is an important distinction, as subject knowledge and its impact on teaching effectiveness and pupil achievement are often misunderstood.

In October 2014, the Sutton Trust published what it has described as its most successful report: *What Makes Great Teaching?* (Coe *et al.* 2014). The report outlines six 'components of great teaching', the first of which is described as follows:

1.   (Pedagogical) content knowledge (Strong evidence of impact on student outcomes)

    The most effective teachers have deep knowledge of the subject they teach, and when teachers' knowledge falls below a certain level it is a significant impediment to students' learning. As well as a strong understanding of the material being taught, teachers must also understand the ways students think about the content, be able to evaluate the thinking behind students' own methods, and identify students' common misconceptions.

    (Coe et al. *2014: 2)*

The report distinguishes between knowing 'enough' of a subject and how that knowledge is used. The report acknowledges that 'the search for a relationship between characteristics such as academic qualifications or general ability and student performance has been rather disappointing: correlations are typically very small or non-existent' (Rockoff *et al.* 2011: 18). However, the report does detail that there is a relationship between the subject knowledge of the teacher and pupil achievement, but that this relationship is not a simple linear one. For example, the report cites research from Sadler *et al.* which shows a 'positive but modest relationship between teachers' understandings and their students' gains' (2013: 19), but also highlights more illuminative findings on teachers' understanding of specific concepts. The report also cites Hill *et al.*'s (2005) meta-analysis of pedagogical content knowledge (PCK) in mathematics, which also reports a positive relationship between subject knowledge and achievement. However, the Sutton Trust report describes this as 'not a huge effect, it is of similar order to the strength of the relationship between socioeconomic background and attainment'.

Monk (1994) suggests that there is a threshold level between teachers' subject knowledge and achievement: that teachers require a minimum level of subject knowledge in order to be able to teach effectively, but beyond this minimum level, the positive relationship tails off: or as Muijs and Reynolds put it: there is a 'law of diminishing returns' (2011: 96).

Based on the evidence presented in the report, some of which shows a 'very small' correlation, and some showing 'not a huge effect', the real impact is not in 'how much' teachers know, but what they do with this knowledge. This subtle difference is often misunderstood as the over-simplification of 'better qualified teachers are better' which is a more digestible message.

The Sutton Trust report cites other findings from Askew *et al.* (1997) and Timperley *et al.* (2007), with both suggesting that the real impact is not so much 'what' teachers know, but the belief system that accompanies that knowledge. The Sutton Trust quotes from Askew *et al.*: 'The mathematical and pedagogical purposes behind particular classroom practices are as important as the practice themselves in determining effectiveness' (1997: 19).

This is an important distinction when talking about teachers' subject knowledge as it would be tempting to suggest that any positive relationship implies that if teachers just knew more, then they would be better teachers. Such a conclusion could lead to policy shifts, such as an increase in the entry level requirements to teacher qualification. This has happened in England, where the White Paper *The Importance of Teaching* (DfE 2010) alludes to just such a conclusion, where one of the policies outlined is: 'Continue to raise the quality of new entrants to the teaching profession, by: ceasing to provide Department for Education funding for initial teacher training for those graduates who do not have at least a 2:2 degree' (DfE 2010: 9). However, what the research cited above suggests is that having a better degree classification is not sufficient. There is much more to the relationship between teachers' subject knowledge and their practice (and the subsequent impact on students) than an assumption that they just need to 'know more'.

One aspect of effectiveness, for example, could be confidence. Muijs and Reynolds' (2003) survey of primary school teachers in England found that those who were observed to be more effective, and to have higher rates of achievement, reported that they had stronger subject knowledge. However, based on teachers' self-reporting of their subject knowledge this could be viewed as the teachers' confidence in their subject knowledge rather than what they actually know. Similarly, Aubrey's study showed that a deficit of subject knowledge is an inhibitor for teachers, preventing them from bringing what they know into their practice (2007).

Hattie (2008) arrives at similar conclusions through his meta-analyses in order to determine what has an impact on students' achievement. He states that:

> Somewhat surprisingly there was no preponderance of evidence supporting the importance of subject or pedagogical content knowledge. The latter includes not only the content matter (the production view so often studied), and the pedagogical content knowledge (knowing how to teach), but also the teacher knowing when a learner does not comprehend, make mistakes, and so on (see Deng 2007 for a most worthwhile debate on these issues). One

type of content knowledge rarely explored may be more critical – teachers' conception of progress in the subject, knowledge of when to intervene, knowledge of learning theory, and openness to the experience of alternative ways to teach the content. These may be well worth deeper investigation.

(Hattie 2008: 248)

The research clearly shows that teachers need to know their subject in order to be able to teach it, but after they have reached a certain level, what appears to be more significant is the way that teachers know their subject rather than what they know. A popular way of exploring such phenomena has been to search for pedagogical content knowledge (an idea that is discussed in more detail in Chapter Four).

Pedagogical content knowledge is intimately bound up with subject knowledge. Teachers are knowledge workers who work with disciplinary knowledge and the school curriculum. What they teach matters to them. However, what teachers teach is rarely a focus for explicit discussion (see Roberts 2010 for a critique of how subject knowledge can be neglected in conversations between geography student teachers and their mentors). This is not just the case for geographers, although it has been noted that geographers rarely explicitly make the case for geography to 'outsiders' or non-geographers (Young 2011b).

Subject identity has been shown to be an important part both of teachers' lives and their work. Ball and Goodson (1985) highlight that over time teacher identity becomes 'invested in particular aspects or facets of the teaching role. For many secondary teachers their subject specialism plays a crucial role. They see themselves as scientists, geographers, historians, mathematicians, etc.' (1985: 19). Ball and Goodson explain that this may be due to the socialization that takes place in their initial teacher education, and that it is akin to subject 'sub-cultures' – a shared set of subject specific values and norms. These may stem from the conflicts and influences that have played a part in defining the subject in particular ways, which Ball and Goodson argue 'channel and constrain the sorts of identity available to the subject teacher' (1985: 19). However, as they acknowledge, some teachers do not fit into this category and see themselves as educators rather than scholars, describing the latter as those that are 'vocationally committed':

They see their interests as primarily with caring for the pupils and encouraging their intellectual development. In contrast professionally committed teachers are much more likely to see themselves as subject specialists and to see their subjects as providing an avenue for advancement as well as a source of personal satisfaction. They are in general terms academics who wish to teach their subject and, perhaps as a result, see their role relationship with pupils more narrowly.

(Ball and Goodson 1985: 21)

The teachers discussed in this book identified with their subject (geography) to various degrees, but in each case their subject identity appears to help them make sense of their work with both the subject and their pupils. This work takes a broad view of subject identity and disciplinary knowledge, differentiating between them and recognizing that subject identity is more than disciplinary knowledge: it can be seen as a way of thinking about the world that makes the discipline 'come alive'.

A teacher's subject identity will be influenced by a range of ethical perspectives that stem from the discipline. Whether teachers' primary emphasis is on the subject or their pupils, this disciplinary perspective on knowledge is expressed through teachers' preferences around curriculum, pedagogy, and their practice. Their disciplinary orientation is, I suggest, a significant part of their subject identity. This perspective is outlined in Chapter Three for geography, the specialism of the teachers who feature therein, and for other subjects in Chapter Four. Examples of how it is played out in individuals are discussed in Chapters Five, Six, Seven and Eight.

It is particularly timely to examine this subject dimension to identity. Commentators have noted that the 'knowledge turn' in education can be seen as a response to the 'anti-knowledge zeitgeist' that has been prevalent in education over the last 20 years (see Young (2008) for a general discussion, and for a geography-specific perspective Mitchell and Lambert (2015)). International assessment comparisons (such as PISA) have changed how national systems view themselves in relation to each other. Politicians can equate 'success' in education with economic potential, and the result has been a concerted move to 'improve standards'. The globalized nature of this movement has been widely documented (Ball 2012), as has the international nature of some of the policies introduced in order to improve standards in education. Within the English context, Michael Barber recounts his role in improving education, and the work and practices of the New Labour government's Delivery Unit in ensuring that policies were enacted and were demonstrably successful (2007). The mechanisms of collecting data, setting targets and publishing league tables described as 'deliverology' sought to make success (and failure) transparent and public. Within this melee of accountability, data and an emphasis on performance, individual teachers can get lost and an important aspect of their motivation, their subject identity, may be ignored. This research sets out to help redress that balance.

The research

The foundation of this book is the ongoing research I have been conducting with geography teachers about their practice. The aim of this work was not to discover if they had a moral and subject-based approach to their work, but to find out how their subject knowledge influenced their practice. Previous research in this field is inconclusive, and within geography education even more so (see for example Barrett Hacking 1996; Walford 1996; Rynne and Lambert 1997; Puttick 2012). My interest in this area began when I was teaching geography and wanted to find out how I could improve my practice. I began my research by looking at the practice of teachers who had been recommended to me as 'experts' (I discovered that the recommendations of expertise varied as widely as the range of practice I observed).

My initial research revealed that there was no linear relationship between how much subject knowledge a teacher had, or indeed what 'type' of geographical expertise they had, and their practice. Instead a more complex picture emerged of how their moral and ethical stances towards teaching generally, and teaching geography specifically, were related to their subject-based identity. I found that all the teachers I interviewed had a subject story that appeared to be at the heart of their practice. This story acted like a form of short-hand which they repeated when they talked about their inspiration and motivations to teach, their relationship with the academic discipline and school subject, and other aspects of their personal and professional lives. The subject story appeared to underpin their practice: it represented both a belief and a guide for practice, and they described being drawn towards it or being guided by it in times of conflict or tension. The subject stories and their significance in the professional practice of the participating teachers were conveyed to me through a series of narratives. In this book, I suggest that these subject stories can act as a professional compass that can guide teachers in their work.

I am not suggesting that all teachers have a professional compass, or indeed that the idea of a professional compass is anything more than a metaphor used to describe the trends observed in the data I collected. Like the subject stories themselves, I am using the phrase professional compass as a form of shorthand, akin to the everyday notion of a 'moral compass'.

The metaphor also has some resonance amid an increasing political rhetoric about the moral responsibility of teachers. In a speech about the moral role of teachers, Tristram Hunt (Britain's Shadow Secretary of State for Education) made reference to the practice in Singapore of newly qualified teachers being given a compass to remind them of the responsibility of their new posts. There is, however, an important distinction between this idea of a moral compass, as described by Tristram Hunt, and the professional compass metaphor that I am using. In this research teachers often used their sense of moral responsibility in order to resist, ignore or protest against education policy or school-based initiatives. This may involve doing the 'wrong' thing because of a higher or conflicting sense of what is 'right'. Honouring teachers' professional ethical positions can empower them to behave as autonomous professionals, but may fly in the face of attempts to control their work.

The professional compass is an active metaphor. Teachers' professional practice occurs at a number of scales: through what they do in the classroom, their participation in school life and as a member of professional communities. At each of these scales, teachers make decisions about whether to comply or to resist influences on their practice. A professional compass can help teachers to situate themselves within these debates and contexts and to decide how to proceed. The moral dimension to the professional compass is akin to their moral perspective, the values that drive their decision making and participation in the profession at these levels.

When teachers are guided by their professional compass, they act in line with their subject story, and their actions appear to become filled with meaning, to the point where the teacher can feel that he or she is acting purposefully. This can be an incredibly fulfilling and enriching experience and teachers in this study have described how it can sustain their motivation (perhaps it is at the root of their resilience and commitment). However, it is a common experience through a teacher's career for this perspective to be challenged, and it is at this point that teachers appear to draw upon their professional compass to guide their response to these challenges. This does not always end well. Teachers can experience great frustrations when forced to act in a way that is counter to their values.

The focus on geography teachers

The research presented here was conducted with geography teachers in the English secondary school system. As a geography educator myself, this where my interest, career and previous research has been based. As a geographer, I understand the geographical concepts, nuances and particular concerns of fellow geography teachers. This is not to suggest that there is something special or unique about geography teachers that may not be the case for other subject specialist teachers beyond their involvement in the field, but as with many subject communities, there are some 'insider' understandings that my insider status enables me to access and make explicit.

Geography is a useful case study for revealing trends that are applicable to other subject areas because it sits across traditional physical sciences, social sciences and humanities boundaries. The combination of physical geography (referred to as earth science in many national education systems) and human geography (and its close relationship to social sciences) means that geography can be seen as both a sciences and a humanities subject. Conclusions drawn from research in geography education can have a wide applicability beyond the subject boundaries (for example, Lee's (1996) work on gender and literacy, focused on writing in geography lessons, has implications for other subjects).

The teachers featured in this research all teach geography (although not all of them would self-identify as geography teachers), and therefore much of the discussion is geography specific. However, the book is not intended to be solely of interest to geographers and geography educators. The focus is on subject identity and, as such, the findings and conclusions will have wide applicability beyond the geography education community. I hope that educators from other subject disciplines, and indeed other phases, will recognize the issues of identity, values perspectives, and the conflicts and tensions that the teachers discuss. I acknowledge that these tensions will be differently expressed within other specialisms but, as outlined in Chapter Four, the debates in other school subjects and phases are similarly located around epistemology, knowledge and purpose. However, to understand the narratives outlined by the teachers who took part in this research, it is necessary to have some background in academic and school geography (which is provided in Chapter Three).

The book is divided into two parts. Part I takes a critical view of how we understand teachers' professional practice. Chapter Two explores the contexts that teachers work in and argues that there is an interplay between context and identity or, to put it another way, that the contexts teachers work in will affect their professional identity and their professional practice. Chapter Three explores the ethical and value positions that can be taken within academic and subject debates, using the example of school geography. This chapter also explores the role of individual teachers in defining and enacting the school curriculum. Chapter Four examines how we understand how teachers use their subject knowledge, and how the debates around subject knowledge are articulated in different areas of the curriculum.

Part II focuses specifically on teachers' narratives of their professional practice. The narratives have been kept separate from the more theoretical discussion to give space to the stories that are told, the arguments present in the narrative. It is in this part that we also draw more attention to the idea of a professional compass, showing how teachers' values can shape their practice at a variety of scales. Chapter Five takes the narratives of three teachers to look at how subject identity can be expressed and understood through the use of a subject story – one that can lie in contrast to the sacred story of the professional knowledge landscape. Chapter Six focuses specifically on the interplay between context and identity and takes two teachers' narratives – one whose values are closely aligned with those of the school they work in and another whose values are misaligned. In this chapter, the importance of this interplay is explored, as is the impact that the interplay between context and identity can have on teachers' emotions. Chapter Seven focuses on how an individual teacher's values can affect how he enacts the curriculum, using the detailed narrative of one teacher. Chapter Eight tells the narrative of another teacher who reflects on how his values have changed during his career. In this chapter it is argued that strong subject values can sustain teachers throughout their careers.

The final chapter explores the idea of the professional compass as a useful metaphor for understanding teachers' professional practices, both for moving towards a deeper understanding of teachers' work and for considering the implications of this for teacher professional development, school policy enactment and understanding the construction and enactment of the curriculum.

PART I

Knowledge landscapes and teacher identity

2

CURRENT PROFESSIONAL KNOWLEDGE LANDSCAPES

In Chapter One, Clandinin and Connelly's (1995) idea of professional knowledge landscapes was introduced as a useful way of understanding the moral conflicts and dilemmas faced by teachers. Clandinin and Connelly represent teachers' work as a series of dilemmas around knowledge. They argue that the landscape is made up of sacred stories which come from official discourses, and which teachers may find are in conflict with their own professional narratives. These are knowledge dilemmas as they represent official knowledge coming into conflict with the personal knowledge of the teacher. This metaphor helps to understand the interplay between individual teachers and the contexts they find themselves in. In this chapter, I want to go a stage further and suggest that these 'landscapes' actually play a profound role in affecting teachers' practices, as the interplay between context and identity can, in effect, 'make teachers up' in that they try to influence not just what teachers do but also who they are. To make this argument this chapter will focus on three questions:

- What characterizes the current professional knowledge landscape, and what are the current sacred stories being told to teachers?
- How are those sacred stories told to teachers?
- And what do we know about how teachers respond to these stories?

A significant aspect of Clandinin and Connelly's work is the acknowledgement that teachers can experience conflict between the official discourses around education and teaching and their own understanding of particular situations or decisions, based on their professional expertise. By placing the sacred stories in conflict with teachers' personal stories Clandinin and Connelly recognize the shifting nature of this moral landscape, that teachers can reside within knowledge-based communities and that desires, tensions and possibilities can emerge from these competing and conflicting stories.

Clandinin and Connelly adopt the term sacred stories from the work of Crites (1971) to describe how some ideas are so pervasive that they remain unnoticed and when named are hard to define:

> These stories seem to be elusive expressions of stories that cannot be fully and directly told, because they live, so to speak, in the arms and legs and bellies of the celebrants. These stories lie too deep in the consciousness of the people to be directly told.
>
> *(Crites 1971: 294)*

More recent work on the influences that shape professional practice has looked towards neoliberal education policies as a driving force in education reform (Perryman 2006; Day *et al.* 2007; Maguire *et al.* 2011). This analysis has been useful in naming some of the sacred stories and attributing them to performativity, accountability and presenteeism (Hargreaves and Shirley 2009). However, it would be naïve to consider that all the influences that have affected the sacred stories have been named. The significance of the idea of sacred stories is that much of their expression is hidden and implicit. The first part of this chapter makes an attempt to articulate some of the dominant sacred stories found in education today.

Another key idea from Clandinin and Connelly is the metaphor of a funnel to describe how policies are fed into schools. The second part of this chapter will explore some of the findings from research into policy interpretation and enactment, focussing specifically on how schools 'do' policy (with due acknowledgement to Ball, Maguire and Braun's (2012) book with that title) and how policies around the curriculum can define school subjects in particular ways. The aim of this section is to articulate how the 'funnel' works, or how the sacred stories are communicated to teachers.

Finally, the chapter offers an explanation of how the sacred stories have become so pervasive and influential in schools and on teachers, suggesting that they operate in similar ways to cultures in that they represent beliefs and ideas about practice and are highly context sensitive. This analysis goes some way to explaining how teachers can situate themselves in relation to these sacred stories and the degree to which they participate in their cultural expression. This final part of the chapter explores the idea that school contexts, and the professional knowledge landscapes they are derived from, have an important part to play in shaping teacher identity.

Features of the professional knowledge landscape

There are a number of publications offering commentary on the current state of education and the forces that are driving change. Indeed it has become fairly commonplace to say that education is in crisis and requires reform (see Pring 2013). Whilst there has never been a 'golden era' of education, calls for reform often focus on particular visions of education's role in future society. One view is that education is inextricably linked to economic success, and therefore a robust education system is necessary for a nation's economic and social health. Another related argument is that in times of rapid technological change education needs rapid reform. Both arguments presuppose a particular aim and purpose of education, and consequently they lean towards particular types of reform. In both of these arguments, the teacher is situated as the object of reform, but rarely as the driver. This promotes an image of a teacher as a technicist whose practice can be easily changed. It undermines a view of teachers as professionals with specialist expertise and autonomy over their work.

The question of how we want our education system to be is an extremely important one. Pring *et al.* (2009: 12) ask 'What counts as an educated 19 year old in this day and age?' In their exploration, they highlight the distinctiveness of 'intelligent management of life' (2009: 13) in the twenty-first century, the importance of understanding, knowledge and skills, and the different capacities, motivations and opportunities for learning. They present a view of education which is challenging and inspirational, driven by purposes and aims which include:

- Intellectual development
- Practical capability
- Community participation
- Moral seriousness
- Pursuit of excellence
- Self-awareness
- Social justice.

They argue that such an approach is important for young people faced with economic, technological and environmental changes. If we are to take this view of education 'in this day and age' seriously, then it is vital to ask what the implications for teachers are. What does it mean to be a teacher in this day and age?

The challenge for many teachers 'in this day and age' appears to be how to juggle an increasing number of demands whilst maintaining their professional judgement about what to teach and the best way to teach it. The contexts that teachers work in are increasingly complex. Accountability agendas, the changing organization of schools, and the inspection and monitoring regimes all impose different value systems on the classroom. Barnett (2008) has commented on this as an 'era of supercomplexity'. He articulates this supercomplexity as particularly challenging for the professional:

> Under such conditions, the professional neither has his or her professionalism given in any real sense but nor has carte blanche to shape it. Higher expectations among clients, evermore explicit standards articulated by professional bodies, and an evolving policy framework developed by the state, not to mention the growing interestedness and even involvement of the wider community: all conspire to orient professional life in certain directions, which may be mutually incompatible.
>
> *(Barnett 2008: 196–7)*

A particular feature of this is the implicit message contained within accountability measures. Michael Barber (2007) has provided a useful account of how the English government used such accountability measures as part of the enforcement of government policy, expressed through the Delivery Unit and Barber's own term of 'deliverology'. Ball (2012) has highlighted how such measures are a key part of what he describes as 'policy technologies': ways of ensuring education policies are enforced and enacted upon.

The 'funnel' metaphor used by Clandinin and Connelly is useful here, as the focus of much of the work on school improvement has been focused at school level by making the success of individual schools public and assuming that change will occur by means of pressure from schools being funnelled down onto individual teachers. To exemplify how this funnel can work, I offer two examples: the first is on how school subjects are defined through curriculum policy texts, and the second through the work of schools and how they interpret policy. Both have an impact on teachers' professional identities.

Subject to the curriculum

The national expression of what should be taught in schools is a fairly recent phenomenon in some countries. In England, the initiation of the Great Debate by James Callaghan set off a national debate as to who should define the school curriculum. However, now the contents of a national curriculum and how it is organized are similar around the globe (DfE 2012a, 2012b; Sinnema and Aitken 2013).

The NFER review (DfE 2012a, 2012b) of subject breadth in international jurisdictions describes the organization and content of school curricula in 11 countries and jurisdictions, including those that have scored highly in international surveys such as PISA, TIMSS and PIRLS. The review reveals that whilst the emphasis may vary between a focus on knowledge or transversal skills, the expression of curriculum content, and the organization of curriculum structures are remarkably similar. Indeed, White (2004) and Ball (1993) have both commented on the pervasiveness of the subject-based approach to defining the school day and the school curriculum across both time and space. The striking nature of this pervasiveness of curriculum structure and its roots in historical legacy caused Ball (1993) to describe it as the 'curriculum of the dead'.

The organization of school curricula into a subject-based structure is significant, as this affects the status of particular subjects and the teachers who teach them. Bernstein's concepts of classification and framing can reveal the different degrees of control teachers and pupils possess over the selection, organization and pacing of knowledge. Bernstein observed that the battle over curricula is 'a conflict between different conceptions of social order and is therefore fundamentally moral' (1977: 81).

In most countries, discussions around appropriate curriculum expression and individual subject and disciplinary allegiances, and their place in the curriculum, can be seen as 'won' and 'lost' (see, for example, Goodson's 1987 account of the making of school subjects and in particular the development of school geography). In England, there have been several reviews of the National Curriculum since the Original Orders (five of which affected geography) were introduced as part of the 1988 Education Reform Act. However, for the impact of National Curriculum reform to be understood, it is important to see it as part of a suite of education policies.

Whitty (1989) notes that education policies can often appear to be contradictory. For example he contrasts the political government's rhetoric of choice in relation to where parents could send their child to school, with the policy for a standardized curriculum. Whilst these two ideas may appear to work against each other, Whitty notes that they are part of a neoconservative approach to education which focuses on both the free market and the importance of preserving cultural heritage. To understand each, it is important to see it as part of the overall policy strategy.

Ball (1993) argues that there are three main forms of control over teaching: the curriculum, the market and management. The statement of a national curriculum and national testing can have direct and indirect effects on pedagogical decision making which Ball describes as moving towards a standardization and normalization of classroom practice. In Bowe et al.'s further analysis they argue that the impact of curriculum change in particular contexts will depend on the capacities of a school to respond to change, contingencies that may affect change, and commitments and local histories that will frame change:

> Not that the State is without power. But equally it indicates such power is strongly circumscribed by the contextual features of institutions, over which the state may find that control is both problematic and contradictory in terms of other political projects.
>
> *(Bowe and Ball with Gold 1992: 120)*

Furthermore, it is not just the structure of the curriculum but also the policy technologies that supported its introduction that will influence how it affects teachers and school subjects (Bowe and Ball with Gold 1992). The curriculum is a policy technology used by governments to control and influence what goes on in schools. However, it does not act alone but requires inspection and assessment regimes for reinforcement (for example, see Isaacs 2014). The statement of curriculum, and the other policy technologies around it, can encourage teachers to behave in certain ways. Within a school, the varied statuses given to certain subjects will also reflect on the teachers of those subjects. These differences are even noticed by pupils (see Paechter 2000). In this sense, the curriculum can be seen to make teachers up. This is not to say that it is the only or most significant form of definition of teacher professionalism, nor that it cannot be resisted or contested. Teachers can position and reposition themselves in relation to it.

One of the effects of such repositioning is to increase or decrease emphasis on subject identity. In his analysis of the impact of the introduction of the National Curriculum, Gillborn (1991) identified that 'The most frequent adopted coping strategy involved a renewed emphasis on teachers' identities as subject specialists' (1991: 15). In other words, the expression of the curriculum into subject groupings had a similar effect on teacher identity. How this expression manifests itself is also contingent on the fluid and contested nature of subject sub-cultures, which in turn are influenced by different models of the subject and how they are articulated through examination specifications (Paechter 2000).

It is not surprising then that when the National Curriculum was introduced in England, its impact was not evenly felt. McCulloch *et al.* (2000) illustrate how different parts of the school curriculum were affected, and how less traditional curriculum areas (such as technology) seemingly lost out in the battle over curriculum space (similar observations have been made by Paechter (2000) and in relation to pastoral time in the curriculum by Power 1996).

> The ways in which the school curriculum is organised can also have important implications for teachers' work and cultures, as well as their pedagogy. In particular, the arrangement and ordering of subject content, the extent to which the timetable is dominated by subject-specific or cross-curricular priorities and the way in which teaching time is divided, can have significant effects upon teachers' perceptions and practices.
>
> *(McCulloch* et al. *2000: 71)*

Such a recognition is significant in the light of what has been called the 'new curriculum' (Biesta and Priestley 2013). The 'new curriculum' can be seen as a move away from a subject-based definition of content around knowledge-based lines, towards what Young (2008) has called genericism (although the opposite trend is true in England and Australia). Sinnema and Aitken (2013) outline that not only is this new curriculum defined through a range of assessment outcomes, but it focuses attention onto the learner, promotes active forms of pedagogy and articulates a view of teachers as facilitators rather than subject experts. These new curriculum models have been widely criticized, particularly by social realists who have highlighted that the downplaying of knowledge in the curriculum is indeed a global trend (see Young 2008; Wheelahan 2010; Rata 2012). But the impact of the new curriculum is likely to be substantial as it is underpinned by a growing accountability and performativity culture (see Priestley *et al.* 2012). Priestley *et al.* have already noted the effect this can have on teacher agency, but we have yet to see the impact it can have on teacher identity.

Any change in curriculum policy has to be interpreted at a local level. The enactment of curriculum at this local level will be influenced by the status of individual subjects within school contexts, the history and cultures that accompany subject departments, and the accompanying policy and assessment regimes. Chapter Three specifically outlines the curriculum battles for geography and the impact they have had on geography teachers.

Mechanisms for communicating sacred stories: the importance of the school context

The neoliberal and accountability measures happening at the macro education level (such as through curriculum texts), can significantly influence the work of schools.

The school is the key local context in which teachers work, and can directly influence their day-to-day practice. Influences from the broad education policy context have to be adapted and understood at a school level. Schools themselves are usually disconnected from the formation of policy (Lawton 1989; Ball 1999), but are the focus of much of its content (Bowe and Ball with Gold 1992), and how schools respond and interpret education policy has the potential to influence the work of individual teachers.

Although responding to the same broad education policy, individual schools do not respond in the same way. Hargreaves (1994) has identified a range of ways that schools can respond, depending on their 'culture of teaching' and how this culture is reflected in school organization and working practices. Hargreaves also draws attention to the sub-cultures (such as subject departments within a school) and the power such groups can have.

For Hargreaves the differences in how schools adapt to change can be attributed to the prevalent school culture, and the types of leadership approaches schools adopt. Hargreaves states:

> Teaching strategies, that is, arise not just from the demands and constraints of the immediate context, but also from *cultures of teaching*; from beliefs, values, habits and assumed ways of doing things amongst communities of teachers who have had to deal with similar demands and constraints over many years. Culture carries the community's historically generated and collectively shared solutions to its new and inexperienced members.
>
> *(Hargreaves 1994: 21)*

Prosser (1999) agrees that regarding this phenomenon as a culture is less limiting than referring to a school's ideology or ethos, as it also takes into account the anticipated and required actions of teachers. In addition, schools develop structures and hierarchies that help enforce and maintain such cultures (Prosser 1999).

This school culture is a defining feature of individual schools. Tyack and Cuban (1995) draw attention to what they call the persistent 'grammar of schooling'. Schools have a tendency to engage with reform for only short periods before reverting to previously dominant and shared approaches or cultural perspectives. Their work points to how difficult genuine education reform appears to be, and this may be attributable to the attitude towards change that is prevalent within individual schools. Stoll (1998) notes that school cultures are unique as a result of their situations, communities and sets of actors, and emphasizes that they can develop as the schools move through phases of change generated both internally and externally. So, schools can have complex and multidimensional cultures which can make them difficult to understand from the outside.

This culture is often expressed through the school's aims, vision, and policies, and by the school community of teachers, students, parents and managers. Influences on a school culture can, for instance, come from the pupils' culture (Reynolds and Skilbeck 1976) and the dynamics of the community (Thomas 2000). Within a school, there can also be a number of sub-cultures, such as a departmental group (Sarason 1982). The combination of these and how they interact together can make up the unique culture of each particular school, which is both time and context-specific (Stoll 1999; Doecke and Gill 2000). However, more recent work, focussing on the prevalence of external agencies that influence schools, highlights that this potential for uniqueness is diminishing (Ball, Maguire and Braun 2012). This is particularly illustrated through the influence of chains of academies and learning trusts taking over the management of schools in England. Schools are also increasingly looking to external education consultants to help them to respond to education policy and to prepare for external inspection. Schools employ consultants to help them with whole school change, curriculum renewal or specific policy development. This reflects a trend for schools to look beyond their borders to assist with internal problems and external agendas. However, the ways the external consultants respond are often homogenizing and unappreciative of individual contextual factors.

School inspections can have a huge effect on the future of individual schools. In England, the effects of a bad Ofsted inspection can be devastating for a school, and many schools have adopted a range of strategies to safeguard against such an event. Likened to the panoptical prison (see Perryman 2006), the fear of constant surveillance can lead to teachers changing their practice through fear of judgement and monitoring, reinforced through a regime of self-evaluation and in-house inspection.

Schools can tap into a variety of specialist support to help prepare for such inspections. Such initiatives are often led by former inspectors who promise an insider view on the inspection regime and framework. For an individual school the ways of preparing for such an inspection are surprisingly uniform. They include learning walks, drop-in inspections, detailed data review, and model Ofsted-style lesson formats to be implemented in all classrooms. This can lead to greater uniformity and conformity in practice, characterized by strictly enforced Ofsted 'lesson recipes', in which teachers adopt technical approaches to teaching performance. Criticisms of such approaches are widespread (for example, see Christolodoulou 2014). The result can be a homogenous, instrumental approach to teaching which reduces it to a series of technical acts, broken down into strategies and activities, without any attention to individual contexts and worthwhile educational practices that do not easily translate into demonstrable learning gains.

It is worth highlighting however, that these responses to external inspection are not necessitated by the inspection regime. There is nothing in the Ofsted inspection criteria that requires schools to behave in this way. The strategies outlined above have been adopted by some schools as a response to the fear of an impending inspection and guidance given by some external consultants. Ofsted has undoubtedly had an impact on the practices of schools in England, particularly as they prepare for inspection (Cullingford 1999), but it does not necessitate a particular type of approach to school reform. Some schools have approached education reform by taking a more collegial and professional approach. For example, schools have adopted the idea of 'communities of practice' to create school cultures which are open to change and (often teacher-generated) reform. Other approaches have included business-orientated practices, highlighting the 'professional capital' of schools (Hargreaves and Fullan 2012) and its potential for 'transformation', at an individual, school and district level. The degree to which schools respond to education policy largely depends on their current situation and leadership.

These changes will undoubtedly influence how individual teachers work. For example, whilst some research suggests that government policies (such as the National Curriculum) have had a huge impact on teachers' professional cultures, other research suggests that teachers' perceptions of these policies reflect their allegiance to other 'cultures' such as the subject communities (Helsby and McCulloch 1997; Halse *et al.* 2004). Moore *et al.* (2002) suggest that teachers 'reposition' themselves within these interest groups in the light of these policies.

Contexts and their effect on teachers' identities

Schools are not always harmonious. For example, teachers can be influenced by their subject department, the culture of which may be different to the dominant culture of the school. Research into how schools implemented the introduction of the National Curriculum in England has highlighted that departments can react in a number of ways in relation to policy. Ball and Bowe suggest that 'differential impacts of contingencies, institutional structures, cultures, histories and environments may produce very different kinds of possibilities of response' (1992: 112). As such they argue that policy texts are 'not so much 'implemented' in schools as being 'recreated', not so much 'reproduced' as 'produced' (ibid.: 114). Further work within geography (Roberts 1995) demonstrates the pervasiveness of departmental approaches to a changing National Curriculum which suggests that policy changes are read and enacted (or 'framed') through durable departmental ideologies.

However, this somewhat localized and sometimes resistant approach to educational reform is changing. The increase in accountability and monitoring through education policies, has left little 'wiggle room' for schools to implement policy in an individualized way. These changes directly affect how teachers work and how they perceive their work. Sammons *et al.* (2007) summarize the impact these performativity agendas and continued monitoring from externally generated initiatives have had on teachers and describe them as having:

1. Implicitly encouraged teachers to comply uncritically (e.g., teach to the test so that teaching becomes more a technical activity and thus, more susceptible to control).
2. Challenged teachers' substantive identities.
3. Reduced the time teachers have to connect with, care for and attend to the needs of individual students.
4. Threatened teachers' sense of agency and resilience.
5. Challenged teachers' capacities to maintain motivation, efficacy and thus, commitment.

(ibid.: 8)

However, as Youdell's (2011) research shows, there is still space for individuals to exercise some degree of autonomy and to react to the everyday 'business as usual' of school practices. The reality of teachers' work appears to be that instances of resistance are 'rare and fleeting' within schools. Ball, Maguire and Braun (2012) report on how policy is enacted in a group of four secondary schools. Their research reveals that schools have become dominated by methods of policy construction, observation and monitoring generated to ensure compliance. In turn, this has been expressed through a range of official discourses of what it means to be a 'good teacher' and a 'good student', which are prevalent and can affect teachers' individual practices. Dominant school practices, and the rapid pace of change, mean that there is 'little space or time or opportunity to think differently or "against"' (2012: 139). They highlight the complexity of the policy environment, and the fact that schools often have to deal with contradictory and complex policy frameworks. Context is significant in how schools enact these policies and teachers are the key focus for how they are enacted.

Contexts as cultures

In the final part of this chapter, the focus is on how teachers respond to this professional knowledge landscape. Studies of individual teachers can provide useful accounts of how individuals are affected but, to understand the impact of these experiences in a broader way, it is useful to consider that these contexts can be seen as behaving like cultures.

Culture is a term that has been much used in education (Hargreaves 1994; Stoll 1998, 1999; Prosser 1999). When used in school contexts, the term culture most commonly refers to the ethos and values prevalent in individual schools. However, in broader contexts, culture is recognized as a complex term with a variety of meanings (Williams 1981). For the purpose of this work, I have chosen to use the definition of culture adopted by Becher and Trowler (2001) in their analysis of the behaviour of academic disciplines: 'By "cultures" we refer to sets of taken-for-granted values, attitudes and ways of behaving, which are articulated through and reinforced by recurrent practices among a group of people in a given context' (Becher and Trowler 2001: 23). This definition places emphasis on two important dimensions of culture. Firstly, it emphasizes the group dimension: that culture is shared and understood by the group who participate in it. Secondly, it emphasizes that cultures may shape action through the behaviour and shared values of that group. The practices are shared because they are informed by the ideology and beliefs of that cultural group.

The emphasis in this definition on values and practices can facilitate a deep understanding of how changes can influence teachers' practices. Many influences on teachers are reflected in wider changes in society or the economy. However, the response to outside influences can vary, and these actions can depend on the values or beliefs of a particular group. Gallego and Cole (2001) demonstrate how the culture of a school will affect how it responds to change and show that this same process can also apply to individual classroom cultures. Using the term 'culture' places emphasis on the shared beliefs and ideologies of a group as well as the practice or action that emerges from them. Kroeber and Kluckhohn (1963: 181) point out that 'cultural systems may be on the one hand considered as products of action, on the other as conditioning elements of further action'. Using the term culture reveals how contextual influences on teachers can share similar characteristics and expectations of practice, as the influences seek to express shared beliefs and ideologies that can affect action. However, this is not to suggest that cultures are static or entirely homogenous, and both values and practices within cultures can vary.

The use of the term culture emphasizes the link between ideas and action. A culture can express what is considered to be acceptable action and create ways for that to be achieved: '. . . culture as the level at which social groups develop distinct patterns of life . . . the way, the forms in which groups 'handle' the raw material of their social and material existence . . . made concrete through patterns of social organisation' (Jackson 1989: 2). A teacher will understand and use the 'cultural codes' that are understood by particular groups (Hall 1997). This may be a tacit acknowledgement but will be identifiable through the actions that they take or through what they produce (Jackson 1989). But teachers may not fully participate or agree with all the ideas of any one culture. The process of developing a cultural identity means that cultures can be contested from both outside and within the group and therefore a participant in a culture may not agree with all the beliefs, values or actions currently accepted by that culture, but they can be a member of the culture in order to influence how it will change. A teacher may be part of a school or subject culture that actively disagrees with the dominant ideas from the broader culture of education but can still participate within both of them. In this way, a culture can be seen as a 'melange of understanding and expectations' (Goodenough 1994: 267).

It is useful to see teachers as operating within a variety of cultures related to their practice, each relating to a different scale. For example, teachers work in particular schools, each situated within a national context which expresses particular values and practices for education. Within those schools, there are often shared understandings and expectations, and agreed practices. Also within the school, there may be smaller groups, such as a department or subject-based cultural group, that also expresses particular values and practices. The teacher may also belong to subject associations, professional groups, trade unions and other organizations which in turn seek to influence education.

As teachers' work is situated within what Barnett has called an era of supercomplexity (2008), they are subject to a range of influences. The broader education culture itself is also comprised of a variety of different perspectives and ideas. Individuals can participate in a variety of cultures simultaneously (Jackson 1989; Hall 1997; Shurmer-Smith 2002) and will understand a range of shared and accepted symbols to facilitate communication between them.

There will inevitably be some blurring of the intersections between the different cultures that influence teachers. Teachers' participation in and agreement with each culture will vary. The landscape of cultures that can influence a geography teacher is represented diagrammatically in Figure 2.1. The dotted lines around

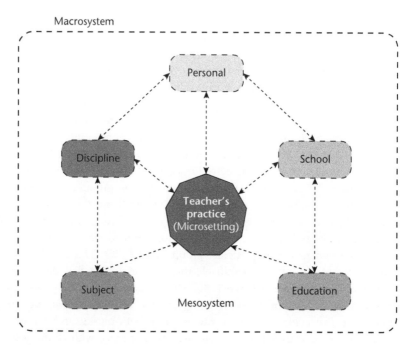

FIGURE 2.1 Cultures that can influence a teacher's practice

each culture represent how these influences are not bounded or tightly defined but are dynamic. Changes in one culture may influence or change a teacher's understanding of others. For example, although all geography teachers may be part of the geography culture (or range of geography cultures), their situatedness within these cultures, and the extent to which they participate in their accepted codes and behaviours, will depend on their individual beliefs and choices and where they are situated within these debates. These individual beliefs may, in turn, have been influenced by other cultures.

Outside of their school subject and its parent academic discipline, teachers can be influenced by three broad cultural contexts: those of the general education landscape, their particular school context and their personal background. These influences can be seen operating at the scale of the classroom and in their relationships at the department or school level with other colleagues, but also in their engagement with wider groups (such as trade unions, subject associations and the disciplinary or social networks). There are some overlaps between these categories and also between the influences of the discipline and the school subject, but they are used here as a way of categorizing and presenting influences on teachers' practice, highlighting their sources and the values they represent.

In some ways, the relationship between the scales at which people operate and the contexts in which they work can be seen as similar to the nested concepts analysis of Bronfenbrenner (1979) in that there appears to be a hierarchy within the contexts. Indeed, as the teacher narratives in Chapters Five, Six, Seven and Eight will show, there is often consistency between the scales and influences on teachers. However, this relationship between the different areas of influence is not necessarily nested (i.e. they do not sit within each other) and a framework such as the one outlined in Figure 2.1 is needed to reflect the emerging relationship connecting these concepts and influences.

It is also possible that one teacher's perspective or understanding of a culture will differ greatly from another's. Therefore, the cultures should not be seen as homogenous or uniform for all teachers, but will reflect how each individual is situated within them, and the individual's perspective on them. Similarly, owing to status or role, some members of these cultures may have more power and influence on the culture than others. This way of understanding the cultural influences on teachers' practice represents a potentially powerful tool for describing the range and extent of influences on that practice.

To summarize then, there are four key features in how a culture can influence a teacher's work:

- Cultures can change over time, and are sensitive to wider social, cultural and economic changes.
- Individuals can operate in more than one culture simultaneously.
- Individuals can operate within a culture without necessarily adhering to all of its practices and ideas. So whilst working within a school, teachers may not agree with all the policies and practices of that school, but that will not stop them being an active member of the school culture.
- Ideas, beliefs and practices within a culture may not make sense, and may be contradictory, but they will be recognized by certain others within and without that cultural group. For example, a school's rhetoric and practice may not be aligned and might appear contradictory to an outsider, but can make sense to someone inside the school.

Such a framework for understanding the contexts within which teachers work highlights a distinction between the scale and scope of influence of particular cultures. For example, during their narratives, some teachers who participated in this study described their feelings about geography as an enduring influence on their practice. However, they also acknowledged that, on a day-to-day basis, other influences had a more dominant influence on what they did in the classroom. In other words, they had to sideline some influences when other pressures became more intense.

These cultural influences can be seen as 'framing' the work of the practitioner in that they reflect not just the influences on individual teachers, and the source of those influences, but also help to explain the way that teachers respond to them. This may help to reveal why one individual teacher may respond positively to an influence and another negatively.

Concluding comments

In the introduction to this chapter, I outlined three important questions to extend the idea of the professional knowledge landscapes within the work of teachers today. The arguments made in this chapter have outlined that the contexts that teachers work in can be a key influence in their practice. The way that policies such as curriculum reform are enacted by schools, can be seen as influential not just in defining teachers' work but also in having an impact on their identities. If viewed as a cultural practice, working in a school can subject teachers to a range of beliefs and expected practices that may or may not align with their own values. Therefore, it is important to pay due attention to the contexts that teachers work in, in order to understand their individual practices.

Changes in education, and subsequently in schools, are making it more difficult for individual teachers to counter dominant practices. Teachers' practices must be seen as a product of the cultures they operate within. Opportunities for teachers to enact their professional judgement, particularly if it stands in conflict with dominant cultural influences, are limited. This does not mean that these cultural influences are the sole drivers of teachers' work or that teachers cannot resist such influences if required. But these cultural influences are powerful and difficult to resist.

This chapter has provided a background to the rest of this work as it highlights:

- that it is important to recognize that teachers are not free to determine their own practice, but that the pressures to respond to school and broader education cultures are strong;
- that the contexts of teachers' work have changed dramatically in response to neoliberal education policies which have sought to centralize control of education and have limited the autonomy and increased the visibility of individual teachers and their practice;
- the remaining question of how teachers can operate as professionals within such an environment, and the extent to which teaching is becoming a technical activity rather than a professional one. It is this question that drives the rest of this book.

3
SUBJECT EXPERTISE AND SUBJECT KNOWLEDGE

The case of geography

Several years ago I received an enquiry from someone who wanted to become a geography teacher and was seeking to apply for a place on a postgraduate certificate of education course. The enquirer explained that whilst his degree was in an unrelated field, he felt he had sufficient knowledge to teach geography at a secondary school level. Since leaving university he had travelled extensively in Asia and in the Pacific region, and had previously spent a lot of time in the USA on family holidays. He had taken a keen interest in the local environment and culture during these visits. In addition, he was a regular reader of the popular *National Geographic* magazine and enjoyed nature programmes on television. He had read the school geography curriculum and felt confident that he could teach it. Although he had no actual experience of learning geography at a higher level, he was confident that he had sufficient geographical knowledge to teach it at a secondary school level.

This enquiry raised some interesting questions for me, not just about what constitutes geographical knowledge but also around the public perception of what knowledge is needed to teach a subject at a secondary school level. A keen interest in travel and a familiarity with geography-related media are not synonymous with what I understand to be geographical knowledge. To suggest that they are, I would argue, illustrates some deep misconceptions about the role and nature of teachers' subject expertise.

The enquirer recounted to me that he felt that the amount of knowledge he had acquired about the world was in fact equal to (and because it had been acquired through direct experience was in some cases better than) gaining a degree in geography. His view of geography appeared to lack any sense of what it meant to be a geographer or to understand geography through a disciplinary perspective. This query raises the question of how the content of an undergraduate degree, much of which is not directly reflected in the school geography curriculum, makes someone a subject specialist? The response to this question also goes some way to explaining the difference between subject knowledge and subject identity discussed in Chapter One. Being a subject specialist comprises more than just knowing content; it also comprises an understanding of the discipline (and by extension the related school subject) with an implicit set of discipline-related values that go beyond content and knowledge. This ethical perspective of a discipline can be seen within teacher subject identity.

The relationship between subject expertise and the discipline

In recent policy texts, the English government has focused on teachers' initial graduate expertise as a key source of their specialist subject knowledge. The DfE's 2010 White Paper *The Importance of Teaching* stipulated the need for teachers to be high-performing subject graduates. The assumption that underpins this position is that being a subject expert is related to becoming a good quality teacher: that subject expertise contributes to high levels of professionalism, and forms a distinctive specialist area of knowledge relevant to teaching. As outlined in Chapter One, the research suggests that subject knowledge itself only matters up to a point, beyond which it is not *what* a teacher knows but how they use that knowledge that matters.

At the root of the relationship between subject or disciplinary expertise and professional knowledge are assumptions about the nature of academic disciplines. Stengel (1997) highlights that the relationship between academic disciplines and school subjects can be complex, and can relate to a variety of factors. It is too simplistic to assume that a school subject is a distilled version of the academic discipline. Stengel outlines five possibilities for how the two may relate to each other:

1. Academic disciplines and school subjects are essentially continuous.
2. Academic disciplines and school subjects are basically discontinuous.
3. Academic disciplines and school subjects are different but related in one of three ways:
   a academic discipline precedes school subject,
   b school subject precedes academic discipline, or
   c the relation between the two is dialectic.

(Stengel 1997: 587)

Stengel argues that the relationship between the academic discipline and the school subject is determined by three factors:

- the relative focus on academic, pedagogical, utilitarian and existential concerns;
- the extent to which the moral is allowed and encouraged to enter the frame of discussion;
- the view of knowledge underlying the whole picture.

(ibid.: 597)

Knowledge and ways of knowing are generated at a disciplinary level. The distinction between what happens at an academic level and at a school level is tied up with what Bernstein referred to as the pedagogic device. In other words, knowledge as taught is different to knowledge as created. Maton (2014) refers to this distinction as the difference between production fields where new knowledge is created, recontextualization fields where production fields are selected, rearranged and transformed to become pedagogic discourse, and reproduction fields where teaching and learning take place. Bernstein's conceptual tools of classification and framing are useful to understand the significance of the structuring of that knowledge within the curriculum and the impact this can have on the perceived values and status of subject areas (1977). But in addition, it is also useful to view the process of classroom practice as a product of the recontextualization and reproduction of disciplinary knowledge. This chapter, taking the academic and school subject of geography, outlines the different value positions that are significant in this process of recontextualization – the development of the academic discipline, the construction of the school curriculum, and the influence they can have on individual teachers.

A teacher understands the difference between the academic discipline and the school subject within their particular disciplinary specialism through their engagement with the subject at a pre-service level. For many teachers this will typically be as a school student, and then as an undergraduate in the discipline. This pre-service experience can induct teachers into a disciplinary way of thinking. For example, undergraduate experiences induct the pre-service teacher into a shared understanding of what the discipline stands for, and its distinctive contribution to human knowledge. This understanding can include implicit and explicit messages about the discipline, its values, the appropriate methods of inquiry, and how ideas can become accepted into the disciplinary canon. Undergraduate studies can enable the student to identify as an 'insider' within the disciplinary way of thinking, and thereby distinguishes them from other, uninitiated 'outsiders'.

For example, geography teachers will learn through their undergraduate geography experience what it means to be a geographer. Studies of geography student teachers suggest that there is a variety of ways that they can identify with the discipline and define the values that they attribute to its distinctive contribution to a young person's education (see Barrett-Hacking 1996; Walford 1996). Rynne and Lambert (1997) argue that as graduates, pre-service teachers have a uniquely geographical way of viewing the world that underpins how they interpret the geography curriculum. But what does it mean to understand the world like a geographer and why is this a useful quality in a geography teacher?

Academic geography

A useful starting point is to highlight the elements of the academic discipline that are often missing from the versions of the disciplines found in popular culture. For example, popular understandings of geography are similar to the view of the subject reflected in the anecdote at the start of this chapter: a Trivial Pursuit, or quiz type knowledge focus on idiosyncratic, touristic or locational knowledge. Indeed 'popular geography' has been treated with some derision by the academy. Johnston's (2009) analysis of 'geographical' magazines illustrates how they neglect all mention of the academic discipline and its methods of enquiry and representation. He also argues that they shy away from in-depth geographical analysis of real-world issues, in order to present a visually safe, but non-controversial representation of a largely rural world. Bonnett (2003) similarly described 'popular geography' as 'an embarrassment' to the discipline and argued that there was a need for a more accurate, more informed, and more conceptually robust representation of geographical understanding.

One of the sensitivities that Bonnett highlights is that media depictions of 'geography' are often presented in the form of 'travellers' tales' which, for geographers, can be an uncomfortable link to the colonial roots of the discipline. Johnston is also highly critical of these depictions of geography, highlighting that they are journalistic in style, non-representative of the range and depth of the academic discipline, and neglectful of the ways that geography can help us to understand the world, its diversity and its problems. The academic discipline as viewed by geographers is distinctively different to the popular imagination of geography.

The difficulty of articulating a nuanced understanding of academic disciplines is that they are not easy to describe and define. Academic disciplines adapt and change, often reflecting different needs in society. Within academic geography, there have been times when geographers appeared to be doing similar things; for example, the roots of the western geographic tradition are often located in the era of exploration, map-making and navigation. Similar studies were also being undertaken at the same time in parts of Asia and in Arabic nations (see Unwin 1992). Such consensus in geographical study may have been due to a mercantile need to chart and record lands for the purposes of trade, but can also be seen in what Bonnett (2008) describes as a 'fundamental fascination' with the world where we live. Such accord is not always evident in the rest of geography's history.

Geography began as a school subject before it became accepted as an academic discipline in universities. The process of acceptance in both schools and universities is attributable to timing, a sense that the study of geography was fulfilling a need in society, and also to the efforts of key individuals and professional associations that were strategic in their efforts to get geography accepted and recognized as an academic discipline. Accounts of this development of the discipline reveal a rivalry of ideas from both inside and outside the discipline (Johnston 1991). In some ways, this can be viewed as geography adapting over time to reflect what society considers valuable knowledge (Johnston 1991; Unwin 1992; Livingstone 1993). But these changes also reflect not just what geography was considered to be but also *how* it was studied and *what* content was considered valuable. This reflects different geographical knowledges (or epistemologies) as well as different methodologies, but to some extent there was unity in the disciplinary understanding of geography as a worthwhile field of enquiry.

Such a unified conception of geography is challenged by different sub-communities. For example, Castree (2003) describes physical and human geographers as speaking different languages. If disciplines are defined by *how* they construct knowledge (Becher and Trowler 2001) then Thrift's (2002) observation that physical and human geographers prefer different methodologies is pertinent. Indeed geography is often described as lying across traditional science/art boundaries (Marsden 1997). Academic disciplines that lie within these boundaries work with a set of codes, rules and recognized methodological practices. Geography, a discipline that 'borrows' from both the social sciences and the physical sciences, then claims to construct knowledge using the methodological practices of both. For instance, the quantitative revolution in geography in the 1960s was influenced by positivism and adopted systematic and quantitative research methods, some of which are still practised in areas of geography such as geomorphology. However, humanistic geography and radical geography (popular in the 1970s and 1980s) preferred more qualitative and interpretative approaches to research. The philosophical and methodological residuals from these varied 'geographies' can still be seen in the discipline today.

There have been attempts to identify the geographical concepts which are key to geography's identity and which form a distinct contribution to the academy. In 1987, Stoddart argued that the common purpose of geography is to answer the big questions in society through using location, position, distance and area as the 'building blocks' of the discipline. More recently, Matthews and Herbert (2004) emphasized how shared concepts such as space, place, environment and methodologies (such as the use of maps) can unify different positions within physical and human geography. A cursory analysis of undergraduate geography texts (see Daniels *et al.* 2005) shows similar agreement on key geographical concepts. Thrift and Walling's (2000) work on physical geography notes that the underlying concepts of place, scale and landscape are also prevalent in geographical research. There is some consensus therefore on the underlying concepts of the study of geography, or what it means to think geographically. Jackson (2006) has suggested that these concepts emphasize relational thinking, a distinctive geographical contribution to knowledge.

Evidence from research with pre-service teachers would suggest that whilst there is some consensus on geographical concepts, it cannot be assumed that geography graduates will have a shared understanding of geography. For example, research has tried to identify the link between undergraduate specialism and teaching practice. Barratt-Hacking's (1996) research looked at 16 teachers in their pre-service year of initial teacher education and concluded that geography teachers' geographical 'persuasions' are often suspended when they teach geography. Jewitt's (1998) work contradicts these findings. Her work on one geography department suggests that the individual's practice is underpinned by values, mainly developed through their academic geography experience, which affect how they perceive school and academic geography.

These observations are supported by work done in other contexts (see Al-Nofli 2014; Preston 2014; Blankman *et al.* 2015; Lane 2015) where teachers' local understandings of geography are shown to be varied and wide-ranging. The relationship between undergraduate specialization and a teacher's sense of geographical identity is more likely to be connected to the values-orientation teachers have towards geography, rather than to specific curriculum content or particular concepts. Geography graduates consider school geography to be different from their undergraduate studies (Lambert 2002). Geography degrees rarely cover all the areas of geographical content that are covered in the school curriculum (Bale and McPartland 1986) and opportunities to reflect on subject knowledge development post qualification are limited (Prentice 1997; Iwaskow 2013). However, Martin's research argues that a geography teacher interacts with the subject differently to a student as the former's position changes from being a learner of geography to a teacher of the subject. Such a transition changes their perspective on the discipline. The learner seeks to link new phenomena with what they already know, whereas the teacher considers the disciplinary structure and concepts differently: this can be understood as a part of the process of recontextualization. Martin (2006) emphasizes that teachers continue to engage with the subject through ethnogeographies, a way of looking at everyday geographical phenomena through a disciplinary lens.

This disciplinary lens goes beyond the geographical knowledge and concepts developed through undergraduate study and involves a values dimension implicit in the development of a subject expert. Stengel (1997: 597) acknowledged that moral perspectives may be 'encouraged to enter the frame of discussion'. Subject disciplines and the way they value knowledge can offer a distinctively ethical way of viewing the world. This ethical perspective can affect which knowledge becomes accepted into the disciplinary canon and which conceptual ideas continue to thrive within the discipline. It can also affect the values of the individuals who have studied it.

Geography has always been a political discipline and geographical topics remain political. Alun Morgan (2012) argues that geographical topics are so profoundly political that they constitute a 'geo-ethic', a particular ethical way of seeing the world. For example, a geographer's view on climate change will be influenced by the research they have engaged with about the causes and effects of climate change and how they understand the issue. This close relationship between their expert 'geographical' knowledge and their view on how the issues should be tackled and understood are linked through geo-ethics. Taking an explicitly global or spatial view of the world involves using a disciplinary lens to view the world. This ethical perspective is an important but neglected perspective on teachers' subject specialism, as it goes beyond what they know, and considers their relationship with the subject and how it can affect their values. This chimes with Robert Bullough Jr's observation that 'ethics are at the heart of the teacher's disciplinary knowledge' and

> knowing a discipline is not merely a matter of cognitive attainment but an ethical achievement, a matter of having embraced a set of values characteristic of preferred modes of inquiry. To teach ... is to be embedded in a world of uncertainty and of hard choices, where what a teacher does and how he or she thinks is morally laden.
>
> (Bullough 2011: 27)

A teacher's relationship with a discipline has then both an ethical and a knowledge perspective which will influence how they select content, their preferred methods of enquiry and how they recontextualize the discipline. It also helps us to recognize, as Michael Apple (1996) has argued, that curriculum is always political, as selections from the discipline reflect judgements about knowledge that are ethically or morally significant.

Construction of school geography

Emphasizing that knowledge in academic disciplines and school subjects has an ethical perspective casts a fresh light on how disciplines are distilled into school subjects. Goodson (1987) argues that whilst a philosophical account might link the academic discipline and school subject derivatively, a sociological account highlights the social construction of a school subject, in particular the role of influential individuals, the lobbying role of subject associations, and the relationship between status and access to resources. Each of these perspectives is likely to reflect a different ethical or ideological perspective. In his own account of the construction of geography as a school subject Goodson emphasizes it as a dynamic social process. He comments: 'Subjects are not monolithic entities but shifting amalgamations of subgroups and traditions that through contestation and compromise influence the direction of change' (Goodson 1987: 64).

Although criticized as somewhat partial accounts (see Morgan and Lambert 2005), histories of school geography have tended to record how this 'contestation and compromise' have also been influenced by wider trends in society, all of which come with an ethical perspective that influences how the school subject is constructed. For example, Walford (2001), analysing school geography from 1850–2000, observes that it has been influenced by progressive notions of teaching and learning that focus on the child as central to the curriculum process. Graves (2001), whose work focuses on school geography textbooks from the same period, makes similar observations stating: '[Geography school] textbooks tend to follow society, rather than lead it' (Graves 2001: 157).

The 'contestation and compromise' in the school subject can also include influences from commercial concerns such as publishers (via textbooks and resources) and examination boards (through examination specifications). Internationally, lobby groups have sought to influence the geography curriculum: examples include the International Charter of the International Geographical Union – Commission for Geography Education (IGU-CGE) and national campaigns such as Give Geography its Place. Lobbying has also come from professional associations, such as the England-based Geographical Association (GA) and the Royal Geographical Society with the Institute of British Geographers (RGS with IBG). Additionally, interest groups and non-governmental organizations (NGOs) publish school geography resources that Standish has argued can have undue influence over how geography is taught (2009). Each of these groups presents an argument for a type of school geography which is influenced by their own ethical or ideological perspective.

To offer a specific example, much research has focused on the introduction of the Original Orders of the Geography National Curriculum in order to understand how different viewpoints can influence the process of curriculum construction (Butt 1997; Walford 2001; Rawling 2001; Lambert 2004; Morgan and Lambert 2005). These accounts reveal how individuals can exert influence over the construction of a school subject and that different perspectives are often ideologically driven. Rawling's (2001) analysis of the school geography curriculum (as defined through the Geography National Curriculum) shows how it has been influenced by ideological traditions, each with different perspectives on the purpose of geography and its role in education (see Table 3.1).

TABLE 3.1 Ideological traditions and geography: a simplified analysis (taken from Rawling 2001: 32)

Ideological tradition	Characteristics	Impact on school geography in England
Utilitarian/ informational	• Education primarily aimed at 'getting a job' and 'earning a living' • A focus on useful information and basic skills	• Nineteenth century emphasis on locational knowledge ('capes and bays') and on useful knowledge about the countries of the world • The 1991 GNC reinstated an emphasis on maps, locational knowledge about the world geography
Cultural restorationism (as promoted by the New Right in English policy making in the 1980s and 1990s)	• Restoring traditional areas of knowledge and skills (cultural heritage) • Providing pupils with a set package of knowledge and skills which will enable them to fit well-defined places in society and the workplace	• Economic and regional geography related to Britain's early twentieth century empire and trading links • The 1991 GNC seemed to stress factual information and to focus on the geography of Britain in a relatively unchanging world
Liberal humanist (also called classical humanist)	• Worthwhile knowledge as a preparation for life: the passing on of a culture's heritage from one generation to the next • Emphasis on rigour, big ideas and theories, and intellectual challenge	• The development of geography as an academic discipline in the 1950s and 1960s and the resulting higher status accorded to the subject in schools • Stress on scientific methods, theories and quantitative techniques in the 'new geography' of the 1960s and 1970s

Progressive educational (also called child-centred)	• Focusing on self development or bringing to maturity the individual child/pupil • Using academic subjects as the medium for developing skills, attitudes, values and learning styles which will help them become autonomous individuals	• The geography curriculum development projects of the 1970s and 1980s (Geography for Young School Leaver, Bristol Project, Geography 16–19) • Emphasis on enquiry, active learning and development of skills, attitudes and values through geography • Child-centred primary education 1960s–1970s • 'Thinking skills' (late 1990s)
Reconstructionist (also called radical)	• Education as an agent for changing society; so an emphasis on encouraging pupils to challenge existing knowledge and approaches • Less interest in academic disciplines, more focus on issues and socially critical pedagogy	• Geography's involvement with e.g. environmental education, peace education, global education, in the 1970s–1980s • The current interest by the [then] New Labour government in sustainable development education and citizenship seems to offer opportunities for reconstructionism, but may only be a relatively utilitarian reaction to changing societal concerns
Vocationalist or industrial trainer (note: in some ways this cuts across all the other traditions)	• Provide pupils with knowledge and skills required for work • Or use workplace and work-related issues as a stimulus for learning skills/abilities • Or use work-related issues for questioning status quo	• The Geography, Schools, Industry project (GA sponsored 1983–91) used work-related contexts in a progressive way for curriculum change and active learning. More recently, government-promoted careers education, work-related initiatives and key skills have been more utilitarian in character (skills for work)

Based on her own experiences as an 'insider' in the construction of curriculum policy, Rawling's historical account reveals the politics and ideologies that have affected the construction of the geography school curriculum. Her analysis illustrates how ideologies and different ethical positions can lead to different definitions of school geography. This observation has been confirmed by other commentators. For example, Marsden (1997) argued that developments within the school geography curriculum appeared to be out of balance, promoting social or educational concerns over the content of the subject itself.

This debate has come into sharp focus in the most recent 2013 rewrite of the Geography National Curriculum, as much of the 'hidden' debate that Rawling's insider account reveals was made public through the involvement of the Geographical Association and its attempts to engage its members in a consultation exercise on the construction of the new curriculum. The process can be traced through a series of articles in their three journals (*Geography*, *Teaching Geography*, and *Primary Geography*) and reveals a coherent GA position to promote a balanced, disciplinarily-informed school geography curriculum.

The debate about what should be within the Geography National Curriculum became focused around how the academic discipline should be reflected in the school subject, and raised important questions about the purpose of school geography and its relationship to knowledge. In one of the papers published by the GA around the Geography National Curriculum consultation, Kinder (Chief Executive of the GA, and member of the Subject Advisory Group) highlights how curriculum reform is often characterized by a cycle of criticism and acceptance (2011). In effect, curriculum becomes as much a reaction to what has gone before as a statement of what the curriculum should be. J. Morgan (2011) highlights that, whilst many teachers are comfortable with the notion that there are many forms that 'geography' can take, what is less clear for them is what the role of the geography curriculum is:

> Crudely stated, geography teachers may experience some confusion as to whether their job is to transmit geographical knowledge, prepare autonomous learners who are able to "learn how to learn", or promote social cohesion through notions of global citizenship. In practice, teachers combine these aspects, but, overall, the trend has been for school geography to become less concerned with the "what" of teaching (curriculum) and more focused on the "how" of learning and the social uses the subject serves. This confusion of purpose has prompted recent moves to clarify and restore knowledge to the curriculum.
>
> *(Morgan 2011: 91)*

So whilst the academic discipline of geography accommodates a range of ethical positions and approaches, the school subject is also complicated by a range of different ideological and value positions around education as well as around the subject. In an attempt to clarify these positions on the purpose of the school geography curriculum, Firth (2012) has called for the community to direct its attention back to the discipline. Firth highlights that teaching geography requires subject expertise that recognizes how the discipline is made and remade in the academy, what are worthwhile contributions to that knowledge, and what he calls the 'generative metaphors' of the discipline. For Firth this is at the heart of what makes up the 'disciplinarity' of a fragmented, plural discipline like geography.

> What is evident here is that students need access to the underlying principles/ epistemic standards of knowledge production, to the generative mechanisms of knowledge itself. It is only through these generative mechanisms that the generic metaphors of 'deep understanding', 'higher order thinking' and 'personal constructions of knowledge' can be translated into specific, actionable ways of working with disciplinary knowledge.
>
> *(Firth 2012: 90)*

This debate is largely then focused on the principles of how academic geography is recontextualized into the school subject. Bernstein (1990) differentiated between the official recontextualizing field (ORF) and the pedagogic recontextualizing field (PRF). This distinction highlights how official articulations of knowledge in the curriculum may differ from how they are recontextualized through pedagogy. There is a synergy here with the tension between the official sacred stories of the professional knowledge landscape and the personal stories of teachers, and it is important to recognize the different voices that can influence this process.

As the geography community has grappled with the problems of trying to define what geographical knowledge is worth teaching, they have engaged with Michael Young's challenge to *Bring the Knowledge Back In* (2008) and have debated what 'powerful knowledge' would look like in geography. The term 'powerful knowledge' was first introduced by Young, as he described the distinctive contributions that disciplines can make to a young person's education. Young argues that schools are special places where young people should be given access to this 'powerful knowledge', knowledge generated by the disciplines that are out of individuals' reach through normal everyday engagement (a distinction similar to Bernstein's mundane and abstract). Young's rethinking of the role of knowledge in the curriculum asserts the significance of a socially realist approach to knowledge – one that recognizes the social construction of knowledge alongside a realist recognition that some knowledge 'counts'. He argues that disciplines offer ways of thinking that elevate our understanding so that we may 'think the unthinkable' (a phrase taken from Bernstein). Young argues that this is 'powerful knowledge' and, as a matter of social justice, should be available to all through the school curriculum. The idea that the knowledge within the disciplines is powerful raises their status and position within the school curriculum. This is the case even when you recognize that different disciplines have different degrees of rigidity in disciplinary structures which can affect how they are represented in the classroom (Sternhagen *et al.* 2013).

Identifying what can be considered 'powerful knowledge' in geography can be problematic as the academic discipline of geography has developed a number of ways of viewing the world. For example, Young has argued that a geographer would view a city differently to a child who lives in that city (2011a). This is not to say that the child's lived experience is not valid or important, but it is not geographical knowledge in the same way that a geographical study may highlight particular geographical features beyond the scope of experience. Roberts (2014) makes two specific points that problematize this observation within geography.

- A child's experience of a city is precisely the object of study within some areas of geography (such as the growing interest in children's geography).
- Geographers have developed a number of different ways of viewing cities, all of which are valid geographically and have contributed to the discipline (and therefore could all be seen as powerful knowledge). A geographer would select various approaches dependent on which dimension of that city they wanted to analyse.

There is a distinction between the way that a geographer examines everyday experience and the way an individual makes sense of that experience. The academic discipline, by privileging different perspectives on cities, reflects an ethical perspective on what knowledge is valued, why and for what purpose. If a teacher wishes a class to understand cities as a transport hub, a site of resource allocation, or an expression of inequalities, they may select different but equally appropriate geographical approaches. The decision of which approach they wish to select is, in itself, an ethical or values-driven decision.

One curriculum project which sought to adopt a disciplinary-rich approach to curriculum development reflects this ethical perspective by focussing on the involvement and perspectives of young people. The Young People's Geographies (YPG) Project sought to combine academic analysis and everyday experiences through thinking of the school curriculum as a conversation:

> The YPG project sought to utilise developments in the academic discipline and young people's own geographies at the curriculum development stage and, as such, was specifically designed to create time and space for young people to participate in a more equal dialogue around the development of a geography curriculum with their teachers.
>
> *(Biddulph 2012: 156)*

A key feature of this project is the direct relationship between academic geography and everyday knowledge being brought together in a way that privileges the young people's own experiences and concerns. This is a perspective taken from a geographical tradition that seeks to value a range of perspectives on the world, and an educational tradition that values the contribution of young people. The adoption of such an approach takes up a particular value position.

In this light, the attempt to create a 'more equal dialogue' around the school curriculum, valuing the collaboration of young people, does not dilute the disciplinary authority or contribution of the subject as it emphasizes what the disciplines can contribute to deepen understanding and take learners beyond their experience. This approach is contingent on the role and perspective of the individual teacher. In the Young People's Geographies Project the teacher is central to the curriculum construction process.

It is this recognition of the vital role that the individual teacher plays that is missing from the discussion so far. Debates over what should be in the school curriculum are important, but the enactment of that curriculum is largely dependent on how the curriculum is understood, interpreted and put into practice locally.

The teacher as a curriculum maker

The relationship between teachers and the curriculum has shifted dramatically since the introduction of the National Curriculum in England. Morgan and Lambert have suggested that teachers do not always draw upon their disciplinary expertise. Writing in 2005, they reflected on how teachers saw their role in engaging in local curriculum development: 'It was as if teachers no longer believed in the capacity to decide the *what* and the *how* of teaching geography' (Morgan and Lambert 2005: 38; emphasis in the original).

More recently, Lambert (2013) characterized education reforms since the 1980s as an attack on teacher professionalism, and he illustrates how teachers have had to adapt to a range of changes within the broader educational structure and organization, which has left some feeling disempowered to make authoritative decisions about what to teach.

The response by the geography education community to curriculum reform, particularly through the Geographical Association, has been to re-emphasize the responsibility teachers have towards the curriculum. Echoing Smith and Girod's (2003) observation that curriculum authors do not have an intimate knowledge of individual students and their needs, the emphasis has been on teachers taking more responsibility for the curriculum they teach as part of their professional practice. This emphasis on geography teachers' professional responsibility has been an attempt to reconnect teachers with the ethical dimension of their subject expertise through how they enact the curriculum locally. Lambert argues that this act of curriculum making must be driven by: 'the teacher's strong sense of moral purpose to inform and engage young people with the idea of geography' (Lambert 2013: 9) which Lambert connects to their subject specialism:

> This is why school teachers benefit from engagement with subject specialism as curriculum makers. It is a prime source of their identity and their capacity to operate independently from the machine. It is an important component of education and one of the means to give meaning to learning.
>
> *(Lambert 2013: 9)*

In fact, in the geography education literature, there is surprising consensus on the significance of this idea. The community appears united in its recognition that geography as a discipline allows for a range of approaches, and that the appropriate selection from that discipline, and the interpretation of the school curriculum, is part of a teacher's professional responsibility. The wide acceptance of the idea of curriculum making (see Figure 3.1) illustrates this conviction. The diagram represents three sources of 'energy' which affect the curriculum: the curriculum (geography), pedagogy and the student

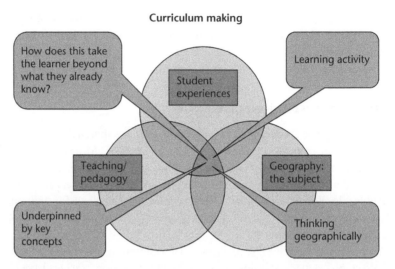

FIGURE 3.1 The three pillars of curriculum making (modified from Lambert and Morgan 2010: 50)

experiences. The message of the diagram is that these three sources of energy need to be kept in balance, and that it is the geography teacher's responsibility to ensure that they are balanced. The genealogy of the idea of curriculum making can be traced back to Marsden (1997) and his observation that geography education can often be swayed by education or social education purposes that can result in an impoverished curriculum, disconnected from the parent discipline.

Part of this consensus about the important role that geography teachers play in the enactment of a local curriculum is a recognition that events at a national level may drown out the need for local and contextualized knowledge. For example, in her analysis of curriculum approaches in geography education, Biddulph (2013) describes curriculum making as part of a process model. She argues that it is because of the level of prescription in the National Curriculum that teachers have a moral responsibility to bring localized and contextualized knowledge of their students into the curriculum making process.

> [Lambert and Morgan's] argument runs that, in spite of prevailing political ideologies in curriculum prescription, and in spite of the influences of accountability systems such as Ofsted, ultimately the curriculum comes *into being* in the day-to-day interactions between teachers, their students and the subject discipline, and it is impossible to have a living geography curriculum without this dynamic interaction. To a certain extent it is *because* of the centralisation and institutionalisation of curriculum decisions that teachers have a moral responsibility to re-present the *curriculum as given* in ways that bring meaning and critical insight to *their* students in *their* context; without this re-presentation young people will be learning inert, irrelevant content.
>
> *(Biddulph 2013: 135; emphasis in the original)*

This has been echoed also in the primary sector where teachers are less likely to be subject specialists but, as Catling (2012) argues, there is even more need for them to draw upon subject expertise.

The focus on the 'moral'

The moral or ethical dimension of subject expertise and curriculum making is a complex issue, often tied up with issues of professional responsibility and ethics. After the original 1988 orders of the GNC, and the widespread use of a single (and limited) textbook series, Ofsted (2005) noted that geography teachers had stopped thinking about the geography content of their lessons and focused on 'delivering' the National Curriculum or teaching textbook content without considering its value, merit or educational purpose (see also Lambert 2004). This approach was termed as teaching 'morally careless geography' by Morgan and Lambert (2005: 157), who argued that geography teachers should take: 'a distanced and critical view of how geographical knowledge is constructed, and to explore the implications of this for teaching' (2005: 156). They describe this as both an intellectual and a moral task:

> Good teachers are fired by the sense of moral purpose to what they are doing: the teaching – *and the learning* – are not seen as ends in themselves but as the means to change people in some significant and beneficial way.
>
> *(Morgan and Lambert 2005: 156)*

They distinguish this view from indoctrination, as it is grounded in an understanding of what the discipline contributes to education and is articulated through the teacher's decision making and professional practice: geographical knowledge and how it is represented in the classroom has a profoundly moral dimension. Lambert goes further to argue that teachers should acquire the professional capacity to say:

- What educational aims are being served by this or that lesson design;
- The purpose of that or this teaching strategy; and
- How the experience knits together to form a coherent whole, so that students "see the point" of learning geography.

> *(Lambert 2004: 166)*

In the light of the powerful influences on teachers' practice described in Chapter Two, the opportunities for teachers to exercise this ethical and value judgement may appear limited. Commentators have questioned whether teachers can be trusted to enact their own ethical perspectives on education or if this may be too driven by ideological or political motivations (see Peal 2014). On the contrary, practising within an ethical code is a key part of how professionals are trusted to fulfil their responsibilities in society. An ethical perspective is a key part of teachers' expert professional knowledge. The question that remains unanswered is the extent to which educational contexts can enable teachers to exercise this professional knowledge.

Concluding comments

The focus of this chapter has been on geographical knowledge, its ethical dimensions and what that can mean for geography teachers. The focus within the geography education community to re-emphasize the agency of individual geography teachers through the definition of 'curriculum making', recognizes that decision making around curriculum, and in particular curriculum enactment is a localized act. It is driven by individual teachers and their perspectives on their subject and why they consider it to be important. No doubt, these individual perspectives can be influenced by the wider debates on what constitutes powerful knowledge within the geography curriculum, and will also be influenced by the individual's own experiences and background. The message from this chapter is that these perspectives matter. They matter because they will influence the geographical education that is made available to children in schools, and may in turn, shape their understandings of the world.

The focus of this chapter has been on geography. To understand some of the debates and discussions that follow, it is important to have considered what geographical knowledge means within and without the geography community. However, the principles are applicable to other subject areas and to other phases (such as primary and tertiary education). It is in the next chapter then, that we take a broader view of what subject knowledge and subject identity can mean, and reflect on how this is understood within different disciplines and phases.

4

SUBJECT AND PHASE IDENTITY

The debates around knowledge and curriculum within the geography community were outlined in the previous chapter, with particular attention to the role that ethics and values can play in the definition and enactment of a curriculum. This argument is applicable to other school subjects, as this chapter will illustrate. Drawing upon Bernstein's recognition of the recontextualization that takes place when knowledge is pedagogized, the first area to highlight is how that recontextualization is understood in relation to teachers' own knowledge.

The Sutton Trust report (Coe *et al.* 2014) (discussed in Chapter One) highlights that subject knowledge matters up to a point, beyond which how teachers use their subject knowledge is more significant than what they know. The report, like other research in this area, specifically refers to this as pedagogical content knowledge (PCK). This chapter takes that idea to task and explores what we understand by PCK and how it relates to the highly personal, values-related perspective outlined in the previous chapter. PCK is influenced by the values dimension that teachers bring to their understanding of their subject. The chapter goes on to explain how viewing this as recontextualization and reproduction may be a more useful way of understanding how and why teachers' subject knowledge matters.

The re-emphasis on values, and the idea of recontextualization, is then explored in relation to other subject areas outside of geography education and within a different phase – primary education. Evidence from a range of different subjects and from primary education is brought together to emphasize that within these communities there are different debates about the importance and purpose of the contribution to education. The expression of these debates reflects different subject positions.

Subject ethics within professional knowledge

One of the most popular ideas in the field of teacher knowledge is that of pedagogical content knowledge. Developed by Lee Shulman, who described it as a key knowledge base for teachers, as it represented 'subject matter for teaching' (1986: 9; emphasis in the original), the term was used to distinguish between what a teacher knew about a subject and how they represented it in the classroom. Shulman elaborates that PCK is used to refer to: 'the most useful forms of [content] representation . . . the most powerful analogies, illustrations, examples, explanations, and demonstrations – in a word, the ways of representing and formulating the subject that makes it comprehensible for others' (Shulman 1986: 9).

The concept of PCK has been very popular with both teacher education courses and educational researchers, as it seems to describe something about the process of teaching which many educators instinctively agree with. Teachers appear to be aware that they use their subject and disciplinary knowledge differently to other disciplinary experts, but that adequately describing that process is difficult.

Much research has sought to define PCK and to find out how it developed and operated. The identification that it was a knowledge separate to other teacher knowledges therefore brought conceptual difficulties. Researchers tried to pin point and describe teachers' PCK through watching them teach and attributing their practice to different knowledge bases, often with little success. Indeed, Gess-Newsome (1999) observes that the research was unable to agree on how PCK is developed, or how it relates to its constituent parts of content knowledge and pedagogical knowledge.

Empirical research in this area started to emphasize the affective dimension that appeared to be reflected in the ways that teachers talked about their subject. For example, research conducted by Gudmundsdottir (1990) emphasized that teachers' values were closely integrated into how they enacted what she calls PCK. Using the example of a history teacher, she described how his values appeared to have 'cemented his impressive content and pedagogical knowledge into the powerful and practical pedagogical content knowledge that characterised his excellence as a teacher' (ibid.: 44). This theme emerges and re-emerges throughout this body of work, with academics attaching different names and processes to the phenomenon. For example, Carlsen (1999) noted that teachers appeared to have both public knowledge and private understandings about their subject, suggesting that these were somehow different and that these differences might be attributable to different values. Banks et al. (1999) described teachers as having a personal subject construct that encompasses their past knowledge, their experience of learning, their personal view of 'good teaching' and their belief in the purposes of the subject. In the work that has built upon Shulman's original idea of PCK, a key emphasis is on the need to understand teachers' values and beliefs about their subject knowledge, alongside what they know.

The incorporation of values and beliefs as an important feature of how teachers use their subject knowledge has helped to clarify some of the conceptual difficulties with PCK. Pajares (1992) notes the complexity of researching teachers' beliefs and knowledge, and being able to make firm statements about the influence of either. He argues that it is not so much an issue of identifying teachers' values and beliefs but of recognizing that teachers have values and beliefs about a range of relevant factors, such as the subject itself, its purpose, how it is best taught and learnt, and its contribution to education. Parajes' distinction closely reflects the observation that the disciplinary knowledge developed by undergraduates is unique to individuals and how they make sense of their subject. But how does this observation help us to understand teachers' practices better?

One advantage of the emphasis on teachers' values and beliefs is that it helps us to explain why some teachers, with similar disciplinary backgrounds, may understand, value and teach their subject with different emphases. The important role values and beliefs play in understanding how teachers develop their knowledge can be seen as incorporating a particular disciplinary ethic. This is reflected in Grossman *et al.*'s (1989) acknowledgement that subject matter knowledge has four dimensions:

- Content knowledge for teaching
- Substantive knowledge
- Syntactical knowledge
- Beliefs about subject matter.

They recognize that teachers' beliefs about subject matter are treated by them as of equal importance to knowledge, with a comparable status, and so these beliefs are an important dimension in understanding what teachers consider to be their subject knowledge. The implication of this finding is that teachers' beliefs about their subject will affect how they teach it, or to put it another way, how they recontextualize it for teaching.

The recognition that teachers' values and beliefs make up an important part of their subject knowledge is supported by research which recognizes the deeply embedded nature of teachers' images of what it means to be a teacher. These beliefs are enduring and resistant (Pajares 1992) and appear to be formed early on in life (Popkewitz 1987; Elbaz 1991; Zeichner and Liston 1987). The images often have a moral dimension which can influence teachers' own professional (and personal) identity and, as such, are reflected in teachers' images around being a teacher. Weber and Mitchell (1996) argue that these images are commonly formed early on in childhood and are enduring even when tackled through formal programmes of education (or re-education). They link their work with Calderhead's (1996) idea of teachers' practical knowledge – that levels of abstraction of images of teachers can reveal underlying values and beliefs about the profession.

Shifting the understanding towards recontextualization and reproduction

Undoubtedly, the teacher is a key focus of knowledge in any classroom, guiding, selecting and representing knowledge from their particular discipline. However, it is important to also recognize that teachers do not undertake this task alone. School subjects differ from their disciplinary cousins and the process of being pedagogized requires a variety of social constructions that take place outside of the individual teacher. It is useful here to return to Bernstein's idea of the pedagogic device and how this involves recontextualization and reproduction. Bernstein differentiated between everyday (or mundane) knowledge and esoteric knowledge: or between the thinkable and the unthinkable (the not yet known). Bernstein identified the pedagogic device as occupying the space between the two, and as making up the distributive, recontextualizing and evaluative rules between them. The process of creating new knowledge is described by Maton (2014) as production. Maton argues that this production of knowledge is distinctively different to the process of making that knowledge available to others who do not have access to it. This process constitutes the distributive rules of the pedagogic device.

Recontextualization takes place at the various levels of curriculum construction. Maton says this recontextualization happens at the 'sites where knowledges from the field of production are selected, rearranged and transformed to become pedagogic discourse' (2014: 48). This field of recontextualizing takes place through official statements of a curriculum, such as through a national curriculum, examination specifications or even textbooks. It is the rules of recontextualizing that affect the transmission and acquisition of knowledge and are made of an instructional discourse embedded within the regulative discourse (Bernstein 1990). In other words, in taking knowledge from the disciplines and making it available for students, it is subjected to transformation. Using the example of school physics, Bernstein explains:

> The rules of relation, selection, sequencing and pacing (the rate of expected acquisition of the sequencing rules) cannot themselves be derived from some logic internal to physics nor from the practices of those who produce physics. The rules of reproduction of physics are social, not logical, facts. The recontextualising rules regulate not only selection, sequence, pace and relations with other subjects, but also the theory of instruction from which the transmission rules are derived.
>
> *(Bernstein 1990: 185)*

Bernstein argues that these recontextualizing rules are influenced by the classification and framing of the regulative discourse: that they are subjected to the status and value given to the subject, and subjected to its own grammar.

These theoretical tools are useful because they highlight the curriculum work undertaken by teachers as part of a larger mechanism of transforming the knowledge under discussion: 'Changes in the theory of instruction can then have consequences for the ordering of the pedagogic discourse and for the ordering of pedagogic practice' (Bernstein 1990: 189). Bernstein is also keen to differentiate between the official recontextualizing field (ORF) (that comes from official sources such as the State) and the pedagogic recontextualizing field (PRF) (which may come from other sources that can influence pedagogy). What then happens in the classroom can be understood according to the evaluative rules of the pedagogic device.

It is possible then to see PCK as way of understanding the fields of recontextualization and reproduction. PCK focuses on the work of the teacher, but that also needs to be understood within the wider context of the ORF, and how that knowledge is originally created (distributive rules) and then used in the classroom (evaluative rules). If teachers' values are an important part of PCK, it would seem logical to assume that they will affect how a teacher recontextualizes and reproduces knowledge in the classroom.

For example, then, as changes in education occur, subjects have to realign themselves to the new context, redefining and reshaping their contribution to education. These debates are often along the lines outlined by Stengel (1997), in her discussion of the relationship between the academic parent and the school subject, and are focused around three factors:

- the relative focus on academic, pedagogical, utilitarian and existential concerns;
- the extent to which the moral is allowed and encouraged;
- the underlying view of knowledge.

How these debates are explored varies in different disciplines, but the emphasis on individual meaning making and a sense of purpose are shared. How these are then interpreted by individual teachers will depend on their own values and perspectives.

In the next section of this chapter, these ideas are explored in relation to a range of curriculum subjects.

Subject purposes across the curriculum

The debates around individual school subjects vary from subject to subject, but are focused around different expectations about purposes and each subject's distinctive contribution. In the discussions that follow, examples are offered from science, mathematics, history, English and art education to illustrate how these debates are manifest differently. Whether the debate focuses on the subject's distinctive contribution, teachers' beliefs or the form the subject should take, at the heart is a question about the purpose of that subject within the school curriculum, what it contributes to a young person's education and what it means to learn about it at school. From this core question are derived subsequent analyses as to the form and content of the curriculum, expectations of subject specialists and how the assessment should be constructed.

Science education is given a high status in many countries around the world. A key subject area within PISA and other international tests, high comparative achievement in science education is an aspiration for many countries. In 2007, a national debate was started in England in reaction to a perceived crisis in the uptake of science subjects in English public examinations (GCSE). This debate was encapsulated in the question 'What is Science Education for?' Published by a think tank, The Institute of Ideas, an essay by David Perks, a teacher from South London, argued the need for a re-emphasis on school science being more closely aligned to the academic discipline, and less about science for citizenship or 'scientific literacy' (2007). The publication then featured a number of responses to this provocation. The debate is an interesting one; to paraphrase, on one side is the view that science education should introduce students to the methodology of scientific discovery and analysis, and the key ideas of the three areas of biology, chemistry and physics. Such an approach requires teachers who are subject specialists, with a detailed specialist knowledge of their fields, who are committed to supporting the scientists of tomorrow. The purpose of the school subject is to induct young people into the concepts, ideas and methodologies they will need in order to pursue further scientific study. On the other hand, at the other extreme, is a realization that a career in science is neither practical nor desirable for the majority of students and that what is more important is to have a scientifically literate population, who know enough about science to inform their daily lives and to enable them to critically understand news reports about scientific discoveries. Such scientifically literate individuals could be seen as having 'cultural literacy' as outlined by E. D. Hirsch Jr (1987). In this scenario, there is less of a need for teachers to have specialist scientific knowledge, but more emphasis on understanding, or being able to understand, the science behind scientific issues of the day (which of course still necessitates some specialist knowledge). The rather broad-brush and generalized view of the debate offered above is polarized for emphasis; indeed many of the essays that respond to Perks' initial provocation are located somewhere between the two extremes, arguing for a more balanced and nuanced approach between them. Many contributors to this debate note that it is not a case of 'either/or' and reinforce the view that teachers should enact a professional judgement that is sensitive to the demands of local contexts. The crux of the argument is around the purpose of science education. Commentators in science education have noted how this debate can also affect the curriculum, in particular in how socio-scientific controversial issues are dealt with (Levinson 2007) and how the curriculum is organized (Baldwin 2010).

This debate, however, is not restricted to science. The Teacher Education and Development Study: Learning to Teach Mathematics (TEDS-M) research incorporated a large international survey of the knowledge and beliefs of mathematics teachers. The survey used Grigutsch *et al.*'s (1998) categorizations of four views of mathematics education:

- The formalism-related view, where mathematics is viewed as an exact science that has an axiomatic basis and is developed by deduction;
- The scheme-related view, where mathematics is regarded as a collection of terms, rules and formulae;
- The process-related view, where mathematics can be understood as a science which mainly consists of problem-solving processes and discovery of structure and regularities; and
- The application-related view, where mathematics can be seen as a science which is relevant for society and life.

(Grigutsch et al. 1998: 210–11)

The TEDS-M study reduced these down to two perspectives: mathematics as a static science or as a dynamic science. However, the more complex formulation outlined above reflects not just the different views on the purpose of mathematics education but also, by implication, on the way that mathematics should be taught – the preferred pedagogical and epistemological approach.

In both of these examples, the purpose of the subject in education influences its value, pedagogy and curriculum. Both subjects are seen as being strongly classified and framed within the curriculum as they are tightly bounded from other subjects and are treated separately to other curriculum areas (although different disciplines within school science can be taught individually or in a combined way). Bernstein (1977) reminds us that these structural issues in the curriculum are intimately bound up with patterns of authority and control. Power's (1996) work is also useful to remind us how this can affect the status of individual subjects that are strongly classified, against more integrated subjects with less clear boundaries.

The issue of purpose becomes a little more fuzzy with humanities and art-based subjects that have less clearly defined boundaries. The 'knowledge base' of these subjects is more contentious. For example, Cunliffe's (2005) discussion of assessment practices reveals the complexity of distinguishing 'knowing how' and 'knowing that' within art education:

> If a GCSE candidate in England shows good evidence of "knowing how" in the way they make self-portraits in a style derived from Rembrandt, this would not constitute evidence for "knowing that" about Rembrandt's artistic practice in a 17th-century Dutch, Protestant cultural context, as someone could be ignorant of such a specific cultural practice but still produce a competent self portrait using chiaroscuro and impasto paint, as Rembrandt did.
>
> (Cunliffe 2005: 548)

Within practice-based subjects, like art, music and drama, and to some extent English, there is tension between the 'performance' which often features an implicit understanding and a discrete knowledge or disciplinary component.

This tension is revealed in the body of research into the work of English teachers, and in particular their pedagogical content knowledge. Goodson and Medway (1990) argue that school English can be seen as having a range of purposes: encouraging functional literacy, supporting students with identity formation, and appreciating how language can shape and control how we think. However, as Ball et al. (2012) comment, the forces that shape the English curriculum are often focused on political and not just educational purposes, and may therefore emphasize issues of (national) identity formation and improving literacy skills. Herein lies a tension between the political values that underpin English as a school subject and the personal values of individual English teachers (as revealed in the analysis of reading in English classrooms by Yandell 2013).

This diversity of purposes within English education is also reflected in the values and motivations of individual English teachers. For example, Turvey (2005) notes that many teachers join the profession because of a love of literature. However, others are motivated to improve students' lives through supporting their literacy development. Grossman (1990) and Hillocks (1999) showed that teachers' understanding of what constitutes knowledge within English can affect how they construct and sequence their lessons. Hillocks' work highlights that, even for students within one writing class, these variations can result in different ways of 'knowing' English.

In England, geography's closest neighbour is probably history, and within the field of history education there are similar debates. As in geography, there is a recognition that many history teachers (particularly in the US) may not have adequate undergraduate experience of the subject (Ravitch 2000). There are also tensions between what history teaches and what people know (or believe they know) about the past, what Wertsch (2000) calls formal and informal histories. Husbands (1996) traces the development of history education, and how (like geography) it has responded to changes in the academic discipline but also changes in education and ideas about pedagogy: reflecting similar academic, pedagogical, utilitarian, existential, instrumental and philosophical purposes. Husbands concludes that our understandings

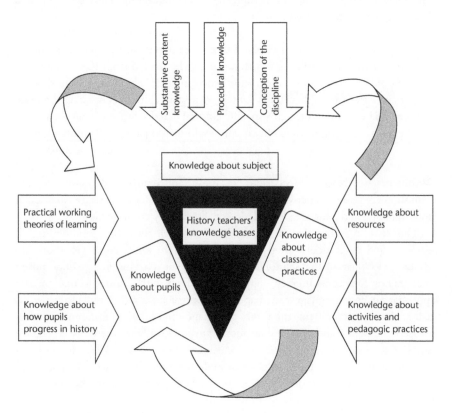

FIGURE 4.1 A framework for history teachers' knowledge (taken from Husbands 2011: 93)

of the past are always constructed with an eye on the present, the needs of the audience today, and that this has shaped how the history curriculum has been constructed. This perspective ties in well with what Barton and Levstik (2004) describe as the most powerful force behind history teachers' practice: their sense of purpose. They argue that despite the existence of teacher education or professional development programmes, or indeed school-based initiatives, a teacher's compliance with or resistance to official versions of the curriculum will be determined by their sense of purpose and their determination to make decisions informed by it. They argue that this helps to explain why history teachers can talk about teaching history in certain ways, but these ways are not replicated or evidenced in their practice.

Husbands *et al.* (2003) undertook an extensive study of the knowledge and practices of history teachers in England with a view to understanding their practice. Husbands' synthesis of this work into a framework for history teachers' knowledge (see Figure 4.1; Husbands 2011: 93) is remarkably similar to the Geographical Association's curriculum making diagram in geography education (see page 46).

The framework for history teachers' knowledge has more detail, particularly in the form of influences on teachers' knowledge bases, but the three main areas of knowledge (knowledge about the subject, about pupils and about classroom practices) tie in with the three sources of 'energy' that feature in the Geographical Association's curriculum making. Both diagrams place teachers at the centre, but in Husbands' diagram the focus is on teachers' knowledge base, whereas in the curriculum making diagram the focus is on teachers' classroom practice.

The similarity between the two diagrams, although arrived at through different means, would seem to suggest that there is some consensus in what they are both saying; indeed, as with the other subjects discussed here, there does appear to be a strong relationship between the purpose of school subjects and how they are constructed in relation to pupils and in classrooms. If we relate this to the discussion on PCK, it would suggest that a teacher's sense of the educational purpose of the subject they teach will influence how they teach it (albeit in complex ways). But how then does this work for teachers who work in cross- or inter-disciplinary settings, particularly with young children in the primary school context?

Identity in the primary sector

If we view secondary school subjects as introductions to the parent disciplines at a higher level (much the same as the 'science for future scientists' debate), then this raises important questions about the purpose of subjects in the primary curriculum. Is primary school geography merely a forerunner to secondary school geography? Such an argument takes a hierarchical view of knowledge, with secondary school geography (or any other subject) being seen as more difficult and more academic than its primary counterpart. Many primary subject specialists would contest this view and the way that it denigrates the subject expertise of the primary school teacher. However, in arguing for a paradigmatic shift towards teaching as a knowledge-based profession, Turner-Bisset (2001) argues that for teachers to become expert they need to examine the substantive and syntactic knowledge structures of all the subjects they teach. This is challenging for most primary teachers who are required to teach ten discrete subjects (within the National Curriculum in England), particularly considering the paltry amount of time devoted to foundation subjects in teacher education programmes in England (see Catling 2012). This view also assumes that the purpose of a primary school education is to induct students into these disciplinary ways of thinking.

Other primary educators take a different view. For example, in his explication of pedagogy, Alexander (2008) argues that the selection of content from the disciplines (a view sometimes referred to as a curriculum decision) is actually a pedagogical decision. He defines pedagogy thus:

> Pedagogy is the act of teaching together with its attendant discourse. It is what one needs to know, and the skills one needs to command, in order to make and justify the many different kinds of decisions of which teaching is constituted.
>
> *(Alexander 2008: 11)*

This recognition of pedagogy as knowledge as well as being practice-oriented refocuses the attention onto the purposes of teachers' work. For the secondary school teacher, the subject specialist, the decision may lie somewhere between the desire to create a disciplinary-literate individual or to induct the student into the discipline or some of the other purposes previously outlined. For the primary school teacher, I would suggest that the educational purpose is differently focused. Nias' (1989) work on primary school teachers' identities suggests that building relationships is a key part of the work of the primary school teacher. These relationships are important because they enable the primary school teacher to understand where the individual child is at, and to make selections from the array of disciplinary knowledge available to help them to develop their knowledge and understanding. This is what Twiselton and Webb (1998) call a 'synchronic epistemology' that enables teachers to consider curriculum and pedagogy together. The focus is therefore less on disciplinary induction than on supporting an individual's growth. The younger a child is, the more the emphasis will be social, emotional, physical and developmental rather than (subject) disciplinary. To extend this argument further, the 'subject identity' of the early years or primary school teacher is more likely to be on understanding child development.

I am aware that this position begs questions as to when an emphasis on child development diminishes to be replaced by disciplinary concerns. This transition from whole-child to subject-based education takes place at different times in different educational structures, the organization of which is largely historically orientated rather than grounded in a particular educational philosophy. In most educational structures the division is gradual, with more structured 'lessons' around particular subjects or themes introduced in the later years of primary education. The boundaries become more rigid as the child gets older.

Subject and phase identity

Subjects and phases have their own debates about the purpose of different aspects of the school curriculum, and these debates reflect priorities in what is taught to students, and how it should be taught. The discussions outlined above reveal the complexity of understanding how knowledge gets recontextualized and reproduced in different parts of the curriculum. As Stengel (1997) has recognized this is due to a range of factors, including the relative concern of the subject, its underlying view of knowledge and the particular moral perspective.

The process of transforming knowledge for teaching happens through the rules of recontextualization and reproduction which are influenced by ideas beyond the subject itself. Other research inspired by the Shulman's idea of PCK has also emphasized the importance of teachers' own values and beliefs in relation to this knowledge (Shulman 1986, 1987). Pulling these ideas together, it is possible to see that how teachers teach will be influenced by various different contexts and ideas around education, how these relate to each other and how they influence the perceived purposes of individual subjects or phases. How individual teachers make sense of these purposes and the way they fit in with their own sense of the overall perspective on the purpose of education will also be significant. This is reflected in subject debates, where a 'sense of purpose' focuses on content and pedagogical perspectives. To state the case plainly: the reasons why we think something is important to teach will affect how we decide to teach it.

The implication of this is that subject and phase identity must be seen as a key focus of professional identity and a key driver in the decision making that underpins professional practice. It is an aspect that has been neglected in research on teachers' subject identity.

PART II

Narratives of professional practice

PART II

Narratives of professional practices

5

SUBJECT STORIES AND TEACHER IDENTITY

The first part of the book highlighted the importance of teachers' values about their subject. The argument made is that teachers' values affect their identities and that these identities may stem from their subject/disciplinary experience and are likely to be made and remade through the interplay with the contexts they work in. Understanding teacher identity is an important part of understanding teachers' work and how it can be affected by the professional knowledge landscape. In Chapter One, it was suggested that teachers' values can operate like a professional compass in that they give teachers a sense of purpose, on the basis of which they can evaluate other influences on their practice. This idea of a professional compass is not meant to suggest that values determine actions or decision making. Indeed compasses point towards (magnetic) north, not to the desired destination. The professional compass is a tool that teachers can use to understand where they are situated within the professional knowledge landscape and how to navigate their way around it. The destination may be determined by the official (or sacred) stories, but how a teacher gets to that destination may be influenced by their other values and priorities.

In the second part of the book, teacher narratives are used to explore what this professional compass can look like and how it works within various aspects of teachers' professional practice. In this chapter the focus is on where a professional compass can come from and how it can be understood. The professional compass metaphor is a representation of a teacher's values: what he/she believes to be right. These values are not easy to identify, and as Pajares (1992) argues, they can be complex and difficult to determine. The teacher narratives shared a common feature in the consistency of the stories they told. When they were discussing their own education, their reasons for studying geography, and their desire to teach geography, the teachers expressed similar values across all these dimensions often repeating the same term for each. All three areas are related to their relationship with the subject: as a learner, an advanced learner, and a teacher. The consistency of the story suggests that there is something here that is indicative of their values, or at the least of their values in relation to the subject.

Determining a geography teacher's values in relation to their subject is actually more complex than it sounds. As discussed in Chapter Three, geography is a complex and plural discipline, which is made up of both physical and social science and can be identified and recognized in a variety of ways. Whilst the teachers in this research expressed a consistency about their stories related to the subject, these stories were not necessarily 'geographical stories'. So the aspects of geography that they enjoyed at school, or at university, were not necessarily the geography they enjoyed teaching. Indeed, their identity as a geographer, or as a geography teacher, changed over time. Their subject identity then is not about being a human geographer, a cultural geographer or a geomorphologist. The teachers in this study had a more complex identity related to the subject, grounded in their early experience of geography as a learner.

As described in Chapter One, this research used narrative enquiry as the main methodological approach. Through a range of interviews, teachers were invited to talk to me about their experience of learning geography and becoming a geography teacher, and their professional practice. We also discussed their lives outside of teaching. In the data collection process, where appropriate, I watched them teach and discussed the lessons with them, collected documentation about their departments, schools and curriculum, and often spoke with colleagues and sometimes family. My aim was to build a picture of their professional practice. Initially, this started with the first interview but, over time, my relationship with these teachers continued as did the data collection, with their permission.

With this focus on narratives, it is perhaps not surprising that the majority of the data presented here are in the form of stories. No doubt, this is an aspect of the method of data collection used, but it is also part of how individuals can present aspects of their lives for interrogation by others (as outlined in Chapter One). Bearing this methodological influence in mind, the similarity and consistency of the stories told are still significant. It would be fair to say however, that not all of the subject stories featured in the interviews to the same degree, or appeared to have the same strength.

These subject stories are significant because they reveal an important dimension of the professional compass – what it is about the subject that the teachers consider to be meaningful. The subject story is used in each of the four aspects of the professional compass metaphor:

1. The relationship the teacher develops with the discipline appears to begin at the moment when the teacher realizes that the discipline/subject holds a particular meaning for them. For the teachers in this research, this occurred at various moments in early childhood, through schooling or formal education, or through a particular critical incident. This early connection is told through the narrative as a means of illustrating the early significance of the discipline and forms the basis of a 'subject story' which is used to illustrate why the subject has meaning for them.

2. The subject story is retold when the teacher is trying to explain how they derive meaning and purpose from their work. The subject story is often presented as a word or phrase, which is repeated to give explanation or justification for

action. The subject story reappears throughout the narrative for the purpose of emphasizing meaning.

3. The professional knowledge landscape is experienced at a range of scales: from the classroom, to the whole school, to wider educational policy and initiatives. The subject story is used at each of these scales and reflects a coherent sense of meanings. Its use at these different scales reveals how the disciplinary ethic can permeate all aspects of professional practice.

4. Throughout the narratives, teachers return to their subject story to show their ongoing motivation and inspiration. The subject story is used to show how their connection with the discipline has sustained their desire to continue to teach their subject.

This chapter draws upon three teachers' narratives. The teachers have been selected for inclusion because their narratives emphasize the significance of this moral perspective on their practice. The first teacher, Paul, offers a particularly strong case of how being a geographer can permeate both his personal and his professional life. However, not all teachers' data have such a strong subject story, and so the second teacher in this chapter is the one with perhaps the weakest sense of a subject story. Nicola is a stark contrast to Paul and her narrative reveals some of the challenges of not having a strong subject story. The third teacher featured in this chapter was chosen because of her relationship with and own investigation of her subject story. Isobel is at the early stages of her career and has systematically reflected on her subject identity as a way of trying to regain her earlier enthusiasm. The cases have been selected and presented here to show different aspects of the importance of this moral perspective, the significance of its presence and coherence, and how teachers can react when they feel its absence or waning significance. Taken together they show the significance of the subject story to teachers' subject identities.

Paul's subject story: the importance of place

One of the first questions I asked the teachers in this study was how they first connected with geography. All of the teachers recalled the moment when they first began to think that geography was important, or that it meant something to them. For some teachers this began through formal education study (such as a key moment at school); for others, such as Paul, the connection with the subject began much earlier and not through the recognized subject or discipline.

Paul begins with stories of his childhood:

> My aunts worked at Horlicks in Slough and two aunts ran the postal department consecutively. And they had all the stamps and these stamps came in in their hundreds and my mum helped me sort them out, where they came from. And this would be when I was 4 or 5 and then as I went through primary school I had a really good stamp collection and I knew so much about

where places were, and that went right on until I was about 16 . . . because of that I became interested in place.

It is this interest in place that becomes a strong feature of Paul's subject story that stays with him throughout his career. Paul was interviewed just before he retired from teaching, in a school where he was Head of Humanities and had worked for 20 years. In addition to his work as a geography teacher, Paul had authored and co-authored several school geography textbooks. Within the school he had also taken on whole school responsibilities and worked with a local university as a school mentor for trainee geography teachers. Throughout Paul's reflection on his career, he described a coherent and consistent statement of subject identity that chimes with this early memory of becoming interested in place. He returns to the idea of place throughout his interview emphasizing its importance in the study of geography, both for himself and for his students. Paul's narrative reveals how this interest in place permeates his personal and professional life and how he has sustained it over his career as a teacher. It represents his 'subject story'.

Paul's early interest in stamps from around the world is significant because he equates it with the geographical concept of place. However, there is lack of conceptual clarity in how he uses the term. In his early memories of geography, Paul emphasizes how his early interest in place was developed further through early experiences of travel with his father who had a railway worker's free travel pass. This love of travel continued through university where he travelled further and met other explorers and adventurers, including someone who had climbed Everest. In this sense, he uses the idea of place in the plural, as places, to indicate knowledge of a range of places, and where they are located.

However how he uses the term 'place' is interesting because he emphasizes not knowing things about places, but the experience of being in a place or, to use geographical terminology, his 'sense of place' (see Creswell 2004). This is a different conceptual notion of place that recognizes that places are contested, fluid and uncertain, and emphasizes that places are socially-constructed (see Lambert and Morgan 2010). Paul discusses how he values visiting and sharing the experience of places with others:

> . . . three weeks I ago, I took my dad out to Dungeness. Because I love places like Dungeness, and it was quite a cold October day and the sun was shining, and I said, it might be a bit bleak and that's the thing that he remembers about it: it's a bit bleak. And he asked me absolutely clearly: 'why are we going here?' and my only reason was because I haven't been there before and I think it's great. He never understood that. He had a lovely day out with me. But he never understood why we went because he thought it was a bleak place.

Paul offers this vignette to contrast his enjoyment of this visit with his father's experience. The story emphasizes how Paul considers his experience of place to be more geographical than that of, say, a tourist or his father, emphasizing the disciplinary nature of his own expertise, his deeper understanding of place. Paul stresses that he enjoys sharing the experience of places and represents this as a 'need' to emphasize how he feels drawn to experience the geography around him:

> . . . when we [he and his wife] go away with other people we find it quite tense sometimes because on holidays or on weekends away they don't always want to do what we want to do. Because we *need* to get down to the beach, and we *need* to go to the end of Hurst Castle Spit and see if there are birds nesting there, and they all want to have a drink or walk the other way towards civilisation. That's gone on for years and years, and when I am with my other geography friends it's absolutely fine. My [friend] whenever I go to see him, we go off to visit an old spit or go up some corrie and we never have to ask why we are doing that, we just do it [my emphasis].

As well as sharing these experiences with friends, Paul indicates how travel and geographical experiences are a key part of his personal life:

> Isolation. Being in places where nobody else is, and one of the reasons might be that when you are a teacher and in a profession with so many people all day . . . [you need to] go off to see somewhere that is a bit more wild.

The connection between this enjoyment of travel and his interest as a geographer and geography teacher can be seen as almost seamless as he describes his travel experience, using the language of school geography.

> . . . it wasn't just the unknown, it was the excitement of travel and looking at the variety of life. And I wouldn't say it was particularly *physical*. I think it was *physical* and *human*: it's a '*people and landscape*'. Some places though, if you ask me about my travel I've done and what I have brought back into the classroom, it would be very *physical*. You know I have been to Iceland three times, and I think in Iceland I have always brought back the *physical*. And I've been to America recently: Lassen National Park and Yosemite, and it's the landscapes, the physical that I have brought back. But in my experiences in the Gambia, it has never been *physical*, it has only been *development* issues [my emphasis].

In all of the above examples, Paul emphasizes school geographical terminology in his narrative, fusing his experience as a geographer, and as a geography teacher. It is also used to reflect a shared disciplinary language, to emphasize his membership and identity of himself as a geographer. He emphasizes that place is more significant to him than the accumulation of material possessions: 'I have worked hard in order to spend it on travel. And I've got better travel than I have carpets and curtains. But then a lot of my geography friends do as well.' This relationship with place (sometimes represented as travel) is significant for Paul. In these narratives, Paul's emphasis is on place as a key part of how he tells the story of his personal and professional lives. He highlights its importance in his connection to family and friends. He uses it to illustrate strong bonds and also to differentiate between those who share his interests and those who do not. His recollection of learning geography was of a traditional geography that he describes as 'fact-dominated' and content-driven, one which was the study of 'places' rather than 'place' with an emphasis on locational knowledge represented through the accumulation of facts about places. Indeed, Paul commented on being able to recall facts easily, which he attributed to his experience as a learner of geography. This interest in 'places' is in contrast to the geographical ideas around experiencing a place – a more humanistic perspective. Geographically, his ideas might be held by academic geographers to be conceptually confused, but for Paul place is a subject story that makes a seamless connection between his personal and professional lives.

Whilst each of the teachers I interviewed articulated a different subject story and a different conceptualization of geography, what they share is the repeated use of a single phrase or word to reflect their connection with the subject and why they teach it. The subject story appears to be a form of shorthand to express why they understand the subject to be important and why it appears to be full of meaning for them.

Paul's relationship with geography (or with place) began before he attended formal education, but grew as he was exposed to geography through school and, later, university. He makes strong links between geography and travel, but uses geographical terminology to reflect that his view of travel is different to that of a lay person because it is so tied up with his identity as a geographer. The repetition of the idea of 'place', even though it is used here with multiple meanings, also emphasizes its importance and how it is full of meaning for him.

Paul's account does have some different features to those of other teachers in this study. What is particularly noteworthy is that his connection started so young, before formal education. It is also the most conceptually confused account. Paul uses these different interpretations of place and places to emphasize what he considers to be significant geographically. His emphasis on place is also reflected in the debate at the time of his interview within geography education about the teaching of 'place' (as opposed to places) and how students could develop a 'sense of place', particularly of distant places they may not have visited. Paul conflates these different conceptions of place with different geographical ideas and presents them as singular and coherent.

When Paul describes the influences on his professional work, the idea of place is significant to him but he sees it as being both professional and personal. For example, Paul has written several geography school textbooks, and he uses these books in his teaching. He describes how his travel experiences have influenced his writing of books which have then, in turn, become his main teaching resource:

> So you will see that we are doing Gambia today [in a lesson I observed] because it is in my book, because I have been to the Gambia, I tend to bring me into the lessons. And I have always seen my book writing as being a two-way

process, planning for my lessons and I have got all my books from the classroom at the same time. So they have come from the classroom and they go
back into the classroom.

Paul also explained why he considers place to be so important for young people's
education:

> I just honestly believe that if they have some sense of place, they will be good
> citizens and they will understand where they are in the world, because the
> lack of sense of place grieves me sometimes. Because they go off to a place,
> and I say 'Oh the Canary Islands, that's just off Africa' and they'll shout at
> me: 'no it isn't – it's in Spain'. I'll get the atlas out, 'Here's Africa, here's
> Morocco' – the ignorance about place is so amazing.

Again, there is some confusion as to whether Paul is referring to place as locational
knowledge here or to the wider geographical concept of place. For Paul, understanding the location of the Canary Islands is important, but he does not explain
why or for what purpose. His early experiences with stamps and travel made 'place'
come alive for him. His desire to teach students about place is also driven by an
understanding that place is somehow important. So whilst his references to place
may not be geographically clear, there is a consistency in their meaning for Paul.
Stemming from some of his earliest memories, and still a key part of his personal and
professional life, place is a part of his subject story, a part of his subject identity, and
a powerful influence on his professional identity. But how does it affect his practice?

When Paul talked about different influences on his practice, he outlined some
interests that had come from outside the discipline. For example he expressed
interest in the development of students' literacy which had been influenced by the
National Literacy Strategy.[1] He described how had adopted some of the National
Literacy Strategy's teaching approaches into his teaching. He also recalled how
his practice had been influenced by feedback from an Ofsted (the English school
inspectorate service) inspection:

> Yes, it was about teaching, and more and more we have started thinking
> about 'is it learning?' now. Even in the last ten years, I remember the first
> Ofsted here. They were bothered about me and my teaching, and the last
> Ofsted here were very much bothered about learning but we weren't all
> sure of that and so we were very much teaching the lesson. They said 'lovely
> lesson, where is the learning?' And we were confused. And the next Ofsted
> to come we won't be confused at all, and we will focus on the learning and
> we won't worry about our teaching.

Other influences from education policy were also significant on his practice, but
could be seen has having been interpreted through his subject story. For example,
when Paul describes how the National Curriculum has influenced his practice, it is
through the lens of his subject story:

> Well the geography I teach comes from the National Curriculum, so it is not necessarily the geography that I want to teach. It happens to be the geography that I want to teach . . . I take examples from where I want, so from within the Geography National Curriculum framework or from within the GCSE syllabus I do what I need.

Paul liked the geography in the Geography National Curriculum because of the increased emphasis on place (which was more than in previous versions), in other words, because it was aligned with his own subject story. Paul describes how this emphasis on place had permeated most of his teaching:

> . . . I was pleased to see [place] come back in the National Curriculum, and we've gone big on place here . . . we do our GCSE through three places: Italy, Nigeria and Japan. If you want to do population, we do it of there. If we need to plot a climate graph, we do a climate graph of there. Before that when we were working out the GCSE we used to have case studies from all around the world. Now we have just three places where we take our case studies.

Whilst Paul may have been selective in what he has allowed to influence his practice, his interview suggests that the most influential approaches were the ones that were in line with his perspective on the subject. Paul has reacted to influences selectively, so when the changes in the Geography National Curriculum or his work with the literacy strategy or his feedback from Ofsted all tie in with his subject story ('improving how students learn about place'), then he readily recalls them. He recounts no counter-influences or frustrations, and says changes in geographical education are as influential as changes in other parts of the education sphere.

Paul's subject identity would appear to be focused on emphasizing place, and increasing students' understanding of place. His narrative suggests that early experiences encouraged him to learn more about places; subsequent changes in examination specifications, the National Curriculum and Ofsted, have all caused him to rationalize how he has been able to focus on 'place' as a key part of his professional practice. Influences from the educational landscape that he has taken on board are those that are aligned to his subject identity and subject story. There is a coherence to his narrative, one that could be challenged for its conceptual clarity but which enables him to make sense of his practice and how he responds to influences on it. It is therefore a narrative that makes sense to him, one that he can defend and that is in line with his values about teaching and learning geography. These ideas have meaning for Paul – they were influential in his own practice and appear to have directed him in how he reacts to other influences.

Paul's coherent narrative of his practice ties in with how he has described his subject story, and which reflects his values about the subject and influences his practice. He describes himself as a geography teacher who places geography first in his understanding and has borrowed from ideas outside of geography as and when it has been useful for him. His subject story is represented (if conceptually a little muddy) with the term 'place', which he uses in a variety of ways and contexts. In contrast to Paul's narrative, Nicola has undertaken a different career path and has responded differently to influences from outside the subject.

Nicola's search for a subject identity

The key aspect of Paul's narrative is the significance of his subject story to his subject identity. It is a strong story told with enthusiasm and commitment reflecting on why geography is important to him and his practice.

However not all the teachers I talked to had such a strongly defined or geographical subject story. In fact, Nicola has possibly the weakest subject story of all the teachers I worked with. Despite this, her subject story still reflects similar features to Paul's: in that it is significant to both her personal and her professional life, and explains the relationship between the subject and her moral perspective.

However, this is in contrast to why I initially asked Nicola to participate in this research. Nicola had been teaching for five years when I first interviewed her. I asked her to participate in the research because, through her work on a Masters degree programme, she had talked to me about the lack of geography in her early career and her desire to increase her understanding of geography within geography education. I was interested to see if Nicola had a 'subject story' and the extent to which geography played a part in her teaching identity.

Nicola became a teacher through the Teach First programme. Teach First is a teacher training initiative, developed along the lines of Teach for America. The scheme recruits graduates from prestigious universities, gives them intense training, and then requires them to teach for a short period in schools in challenging circumstances. Nicola chose this route because she felt it was the most prestigious route into teaching and was the most challenging to get into:

> I think I have always challenged myself and wanted to do something that was difficult . . . I don't pick the easy routes I guess and I want to do what I perceive as being the best. So going to a good university, having a good job, and I think with Teach First it made it a bit more competitive, whereas I didn't see teaching through the PGCE route as being competitive; I thought it was something that a lot of people could do.

After two years teaching in a challenging school, as part of the Teach First scheme, Nicola then moved to a new school. Nicola's new school was an academy that had been 'transformed' by the Headteacher and that had been described as 'outstanding' in its latest Ofsted inspection. The Headteacher of Nicola's school had been singled out for praise as to how she had transformed the school, and had received publicity for her work in education policy. Nicola outlined that she felt that she had learnt all she could in her first school, and had moved to the new school in order to develop and improve her practice. Nicola is reflective about what she had learnt in this new school context, and the importance of strong school leadership:

Gender, ethnicity, ability: it is a very diverse school. And there are students who have a lot of issues. But the difference is that most of the time they leave them at the gate, and they don't bring them into the school. I think because there are good policies and a clear Head, and the fact that everyone sticks to the same rules and the kids know the expectations of them. I can see how it should be done. The issues with the other school – when I was there I didn't necessarily realise what they were and it was actually that there was no-one leading at the top. Whereas now I can see what might have been needed to be done to improve.

The transformation of her current school was achieved through strong leadership which had increased the monitoring of individual teachers. Nicola reflected on the impact this had on her practice and, whilst acknowledging that the workload was heavy, she considered these mechanisms to be important for her own professionalism as well as for the students:

In my last school, I felt like I was the only person who marked any books, but there was no-one checking on what you were doing and you didn't have to do it to a high standard. You were just left to do it. Whereas here it is monitored and you have to follow the school marking policy, which when you have ten classes is quite hard to maintain . . . in my first school the pressure was just mainly put on by myself and what I wanted to achieve and how I wanted to help the pupils, whereas now there's a lot of external pressure that affects my role.

Nicola responds positively to this high degree of monitoring, and enjoys the challenge it offers her and her practice. Whilst the example given above is grounded in a school policy, it reflects a wider trend in the culture of education in England for increased teacher accountability and monitoring. Nicola is broadly in favour of these approaches because she can see their value for her own practice, particularly in comparison to her previous school experience.

Nicola described a desire to become a better teacher:

I did the two Teach First years there [at her first school] and then I left because I wanted to see how it should be done. I felt that I had developed my teaching strategies and my behaviour management strategies but in terms of being able to *make a difference* to the bigger picture, I felt I needed to see how it should be done because I didn't think I had enough experience [my emphasis].

This idea of 'making a difference' indicates that Nicola is not only seeking to improve her own practice but is also conscious that such self-development has an impact on her students and within the wider context of the school:

Towards the end of my two years there I felt like I was *making a difference* to their geography lessons, and they would behave whilst they were in my lessons, but their whole school experience . . . the other classrooms they went to, they had a very negative experience of learning so I felt that apart from within my little bubble there wasn't really *much of an impact* of what I could have done and even within my bubble there wasn't much support and links between other areas – there was a very limited amount that I felt I could do that was helpful [my emphasis].

Nicola's professional identity appears to be orientated around being a teacher rather than a geographer. Nicola's identity as a geographer is not as strong as Paul's or some of the other teachers featured in this research. She does not identify herself as a geographer to the same extent.

I actually didn't intend to study geography at university. I applied to do natural sciences at university and I was going to do chemistry, psychology and a little bit of geography. When I got to [university] – it didn't fit into the timetable like that, so I ended up doing geography and anthropology instead. So I kind of fell into it but now I can't imagine being a chemistry teacher.

She clearly enjoys geographical pursuits: 'I think travelling and seeing different places has made that interest grow within me.' This wider experience of the world has influenced why she thinks that it is important to study geography:

At university I did mostly physical geography whereas now that isn't really what I am interested in. I do think that my travelling has affected my views on geography quite a lot and the importance of studying geography. In the world we are living in more students will have the opportunity to travel. Or the school where I teach in – it is very multicultural and I think it is important they have an understanding of different parts of the world and different cultures and different places and maybe that's even part of teaching in a multicultural school – and maybe that's part of the reason that I've got more interested in it. As geography in a lot of the older textbooks is a very Western view of the world and I think it is very important to teach them a more balanced view of the world.

In our discussions, this is the closest that Nicola gets to articulating a subject identity. The motivation, like her desire to improve her own practice, is orientated around improving the experience and understanding of her students. It positions geography as a resource that students can use to improve their understanding of the world. The emphasis is on her own development and on her students, rather than on the subject. Her subject story then is about situating students' understanding within their experience of the world. It is less geographical than Paul's emphasis on place, but has a strong moral dimension.

Nicola's subject story can be seen as being about helping students to understand the world better. It is not about geography in itself but uses geography as a means to an end. This is a parallel to her own relationship with geography as that was a means to an end for her (to become a teacher). This does not mean she is not committed to the subject or to teaching, but that she has not been required to place emphasis on this subject dimension.

Nicola talked to me about her relationship with the subject, and how she felt this was something that she wanted to develop in her own practice. Nicola described herself as being 'secure' in her subject knowledge, in that she felt that her undergraduate degree had adequately covered all she needed to know about geographical content. However, her initial teacher preparation did not have a strong subject component and she felt there were aspects of her subject-specific expertise that were lacking: her further elaboration indicated that this was possibly around subject specific pedagogy (or perhaps pedagogical content knowledge, see Chapter Three). It was at this point that she enrolled on a Masters degree programme and she described the impact the programme had on her practice:

> I think it has made me question smaller things like using images in my lessons – why am I using certain images – and bigger things like what is the purpose behind teaching certain things. It has made me question more about what I am actually teaching rather than how I am teaching it I guess . . . before, it was all about trying to get them engaged and motivated and whereas now I am concentrating more on how to make them learn and what I actually want them to learn and get out of my lessons rather than just having a fun time.

Whilst Nicola's identity clearly has a strong moral dimension (the desire to 'make a difference') this was not necessarily grounded in her subject identity, but in her desire to be a better teacher. However, she identifies this as a weakness in her own practice, and has identified it as an area for development. It is as though Nicola herself has realized that she needs a stronger subject identity to develop further in her teaching. She is a sharp contrast to Paul and his more traditional and autonomous professionalism. But, placed side-by-side, we can see that whilst they have very different paths and motivations, they share an alignment between their own motivations and how they respond to influences from the broader educational context. For Paul the trends in education were something he could view selectively: extracting from them the areas that would help him to teach geography in the way that he thought it should be done. Nicola viewed the broader education culture positively, and saw how some initiatives, like increased monitoring, could be used to benefit students. Nicola's motivations were more about being a teacher than promoting a particular type of geography. It is possible of course that, through experience, Nicola will become as selective as Paul; however, both narratives show a consistency between the values of the teacher, their subject identity and subject story and how they respond to influences from the education culture. They have focused on how the influences have been in alignment with their own motivations or identity. Each is expressed as a moral imperative.

The consistency suggests a commonality and alignment between shared values and practice. Nicola and Paul have outlined areas where the broader educational culture and their own identity share similar values and purposes. It is here that they can articulate their views safely: when their own identities and those of the initiatives appear to be aligned. But what happens when a teacher's subject identity and the broader education culture of influences are not aligned? What happens when they pull in different directions? The next teacher's narrative, that of Isobel, explores this scenario.

The significance of the subject story

I do not want to give the impression that having a subject story is somehow automatic or even easy. In fact, many of the teachers in this research who were at the earlier stages of their careers found it difficult to maintain their sense of purpose in the melee of school life. The problems of early career teachers are well documented (see Sammons *et al.* 2007), and support is often made available to them. However, whilst most of this support is of a practical nature and emphasizes coping skills, it does not address some of the problems that many early career teachers face, which can also be seen as the lack of opportunity to express or engage with their professional compass.

Exploring the challenges of early career teachers can help to reveal the importance of their subject identities in the development of their emerging professional identities. Isobel had been teaching for three years, and was conscious that her own motivation to teach was waning. It was this concern that prompted her to make her own practice a feature of her dissertation research, and it is her auto-ethnographic research into her own practice that provides the data for the remainder of this chapter. She recounts: 'Three years into my career, the reality of teaching has meant the idealism I entered the profession with has significantly diminished. Although I still view myself as committed, I do not always feel effective.' Using this as her motivation, Isobel conducted a piece of auto-ethnographic research to determine her own subject identity, the other influences on her practice and how these were aligned. Her dissertation makes for sobering reading, and extracts are included here as she outlines her own auto-ethnographic analysis.

Recalling significant influences in her childhood and in learning geography, Isobel describes her subject identity:

> The findings suggest my identity as a geographer has been (and continues to be) shaped by a number of influences, from travel, formal education and the media. The findings also reflect the importance I place on 'being a geographer'. I conclude that my geographical identity is aligned with the reconstructionist ideology. The influence of geography on my life and the importance that I place on it suggest I see great value in the discipline as an instrument for change in an increasingly complex world.

By describing her subject identity as aligned with the reconstructionist ideology, Isobel is drawing upon the ideological traditions outlined by Rawling (2001) (see Table 3.1 in Chapter Three).

Like Paul, Isobel's interest in geography began early in life, but for Isobel it stemmed from her early formal education. She reflects that her early interest in geography, started when she tried to save a polluted local stream whilst in primary school. This later developed when she undertook environmental conservation work during her gap year. A theme in Isobel's subject identity is the desire to change the world, and to 'fix' environmental problems. This is aligned with her desire to teach geography, as she feels that young people should have an understanding of human-environment interactions. In her desire to meet these aims, Isobel views influences from the school and from education policies and trends in terms of whether they help her to meet these aims for geography education, or get in the way.

Isobel's analysis of education and school cultures reflects that the influences from her school have been mixed and she largely attributes this to a heavy workload. Isobel's interpretation is that this workload has been characterized by the school responding to external agendas in education policies. She therefore attributes most of the negative influences on her practice as stemming from the broader education culture, putting, as she suggests, her professional identity 'at risk'.

There are two main themes that she recognizes as having emerged from this broader education culture: one is the impact of Ofsted. In Isobel's own words:

> A key influence within the education culture is Ofsted . . . Our school was last inspected in 2009 and so for the past academic year there has been distinct nervousness amongst senior management about a forthcoming visit. Whilst most of the pressure is simply to do things we are doing anyway, the constant reminders become a little draining. This pressure contributes to negative feelings about how effective I am being.

> Comments from senior management in briefing left me feeling overwhelmed and ineffective about the work I had to do. This also meant that my time became directed away from planning and supporting exam groups to marking exercise books.

One of the outcomes of the senior leadership team's anxiety was the instigation of learning walks. Learning walks are a commonly used practice in schools, where members of the senior leadership team walk around the school, 'dropping in' to lessons unannounced to see snapshots of practice. Isobel describes the effects:

> Another instance that left me questioning my efficacy was the introduction of no notice 'learning walks' around the time OFSTED was expected. In principle, I think this is an excellent idea, as it would support teaching and learning if done routinely. However, this was not the case and the students were not used to it. On one occasion, a student was questioned about a target written by another student on some peer-assessed work. He said he did not understand the target, which the senior teacher in the room then pointed out to me whilst I was in the middle of teaching. As it happened, my lesson that day

was solely focused on the principles of good targets and feedback; however, I was left feeling inadequate after the comments made by the observer.

Isobel's reaction to this observation reveals how committed she is to her practice, and how she felt that external measures, and the way they were being interpreted by the school, were not helping her to achieve her goals.

Ofsted was not the only pressure on Isobel's practice. The changing examination structure also exerted significant pressure. In her dissertation she recalls:

> Government policy is a significant area of education culture that influences teachers' practice. Recent changes to the examination system in England have led to greater pressure on teachers to revise existing schemes of work. We follow the AQA B Geography GCSE specification, which changed this year to address concerns from government about the breadth and depth of previous qualifications (OFQUAL 2013). Whilst the intention of this was to make the examination more rigorous, the only real change I could observe was an increase in content to be learnt, a reflection perhaps on the cultural restorationist ideology of the current administration (Rawling 2001). The changes were accredited late in the summer of 2012 and resulted in a new module of work having to be resourced in September 2012, placing additional pressures on the department and removal of focus from elsewhere. Implementing reform like this 'onto' teachers with short notice and limited support is likely to lead to work overload and subsequently an increase in the instability and decline in commitment of teachers.

Isobel was becoming personally affected by these changes in education, as she recounted in her interview:

> I find listening to Michael Gove [the then Secretary of State for Education] very demoralising 'cause its usually something I'll hear on the radio at 7 at night when I'm coming home after having been there 12 hours and I'll just think 'are you joking, please come and shadow me for the day and then tell me I'm failing whatever students the most, come and sit in my year 9 lesson and just understand'.

In trying to understand this problem, Isobel recalls in her dissertation that she found it helpful to contrast her own 'ideology' with that of the educational culture that she finds herself in, noting how they are misaligned:

> The discussion above highlights some of the impacts that the education culture has had on my practice and identity. In this case, this influence is negative, which can be attributed to the conflict between my reconstructionist view of education and the restorationist ideology of the current administration (Rawling, 2001).

Her systematic reflection also notes how this has changed over time:

> I found that the influence of my geographical identity was inconsistent across my career so far. For example, my initial experiences in teaching reflected a dominance of my geographical identity (and perhaps of the geography culture), with the production of visual lessons based on personal experiences. This was attributed to the support obtained in nurturing my geographical identity through university-based postgraduate training.
>
> As other cultures have become more dominant in my practice in the first two years of my career, this has led to a declining influence of my geographical identity. Towards the end of my third year, I have seen a renewed engagement with my identity, perhaps because of undertaking research which has meant that the geography education culture has become more dominant.
>
> I have found that adopting relevant issues for discussion has led to greater engagement of students in my lessons. Incorporation of my subject identity once more has helped me to negotiate my practice with greater confidence.

For Isobel, the act of systematically researching this area of her practice made her subject identity more evident to her. Such a reorientation had a significant impact on her practice and motivation. Isobel does not use the term 'subject story' herself, but her analysis shows how motivating it can be to rediscover a sense of subject identity. The narrative approach is not about determining the narrative but about understanding its meaning. So although Isobel has already presented this for assessment, it really does reflect narrative as argument, as the argument was generated for scrutiny and judgement. In that sense it can be seen as having 'worked up' a story to a more refined and polished narrative.

Taken at face value, it is a depressing story of how a teacher can feel pressurized by changes in their education context and school policies, particularly when they put their professional identity at risk. But Isobel's story can also help us to understand how the subject story interacts with the professional knowledge landscape. In Isobel's self analysis she presents how one (the sacred story) is dominating the other (her subject identity) and how, through her time reflecting on this, she has found it useful to reconnect with her subject story.

In all the cases presented here, there is a moral imperative. For Paul, place is a key part of a young person's education – an essential component. For Nicola the subject is a means to an end, one that she recognizes is key to her own development and reflection. For Isobel, the subject is being put at risk through a variety of other pressures and influences being exerted on her.

Why are these moral aspects so important?

The three teachers discussed in this chapter have all shown very different subject identities. Paul and Nicola have different values and beliefs about teaching geography but they have been selective about what aspects of the influences outside of the subject have influenced their professional practice, and have sought to emphasize the positive influences. In Isobel's case, however, the experience has been much less positive, which she attributes to a conflict between her 'subject story' and that of the dominant education culture as she sees it. Each of the narratives offers a different insight into the practice of these teachers and how they make sense of the influences that form the broad education culture around them.

For Paul, we can see the sustaining and nourishing influence of having a strongly worked out and coherent 'subject story'. Paul can trace this from his childhood through to his current practice, and he uses it as a lens through which he can be selective about educational policy. The notion of 'place', as he uses it, may have some conflicting conceptual ideas within it, but for Paul it has coherence and meaning; it guides his sense of why he is teaching and the importance of his students learning geography. His narrative also recounts how he has been influenced by the education culture around him – where the values of the two are aligned.

Nicola adopts a different approach that reflects her idea of professional practice. The subject dimension of her story is less strong, but no less consistent. Seeing herself as an autonomous professional, she understands that geography can support her students to 'understand their world'. She views the changes influenced by the broader education culture as opportunities, both for herself and for her students, and adapts to them in order to get the best out of them. She wants to learn from them about the 'best' approaches to teaching and education and this is reflected in the development of her career. In both of these narratives there are shared values and understandings between the individual and the broader education culture. These have strong moral dimensions, and are aligned to their purposes of education. In both cases, there is an alignment between the subject story and how they perceive education.

The third teacher in this chapter, Isobel, tells a different story. Isobel blames the educational system for reducing her motivation to teach. In Isobel's case it is only through conducting research into her professional practice that she rediscovered her subject identity and reengaged with it. She highlights that this has had an invigorating effect on her emotions and passion for teaching.

Taken together, the three teachers' narratives suggest that subject identity can act as a key driver in how teachers respond to the education culture around them. They described their subject story as being consistent across areas of their practice, from their initial interest in the subject they teach, through to their initial and continuing desire to teach that subject. However, subject identity is not always static. Isobel shows how it can get sidelined in the day to day business of practice and other influences. Nicola discusses how she wishes to develop it further. However, in all cases subject identity appears to share some key features:

- The subject story begins at the moment when the subject starts to have particular meaning for the teacher. For Paul this was early on in his childhood; for other teachers it can occur much later.
- The subject story reflects a particular element of meaning for that teacher. This may be a recollection from which personal meaning is derived, or a story that is told to outline a particular value or perspective.

- Despite the changing contexts, the teacher keeps returning to the subject story as a way of articulating why they maintain a relationship with the subject.

As with the three teachers in this chapter, the degree and strength of subject story can vary enormously. When the subject story is strong, it appears to have great meaning for the teacher and to continue to sustain them as learners and as teachers of that subject.

In the three narratives presented here, there are three different and separate subject stories: each representing values about the subject and its contribution to education. The narratives also show that these perspectives are influential in how the teachers have responded to the education culture around them. It is this relationship that is at the heart of the professional compass metaphor. The subject stories appear to be very influential, and deeply engrained. The influence of these subject stories is significant, but not always predictable. In other words, having a subject story is not the same as having a professional compass: understanding why the subject is significant is part of developing a professional identity. But once a teacher has such a significant expression of subject identity, it can affect how they respond to other influences around them: it can affect the interplay between context and identity. The narratives in this chapter looked at professional practice broadly. In the chapter that follows, we look specifically at the how this interplay between context and identity can work within particular school cultures.

Notes

1 The Literacy Strategy was introduced by the government in 1998 to improve the teaching of literacy in schools.

6
NAVIGATING AND FORMING SCHOOL CULTURES

In the previous chapter, the emphasis was placed on teachers' subject stories as an expression of their identity. However, as noted in the first part of this book, teachers' identities are not static entities. The contexts that teachers work in are hugely influential in how teachers see themselves. Fang (1996) calls this the consistency and inconsistency tension: on one hand, research suggests that identities are fixed and enduring; on the other hand, identities are constructed in relation to where a teacher works. In this chapter, I explore the interplay between context and identity and how that can affect the extent to which an individual's values are aligned or misaligned with those of the contexts they work in.

It is important here to distinguish between a teacher's identity and the sense of self. Beauchamp and Thomas (2009) argue that self is central to shaping and re-shaping teacher identity in relation to professional contexts. They argue that this is because our concept of self is made up of our 'actual self' (who we are), our 'ought self' (how we feel we should be) and our 'ideal self' (what we want to be). As such the relationship between identity and self is tied up with public and private perceptions. Beauchamp and Thomas distinguish between the process (the self) and product (the identity). 'Self' can be seen as highly emotional, personal and internal to the individual, whereas identity is achieved through a process of becoming and is significantly influenced by context.

The idiosyncratic nature of how teachers respond to contexts is influenced by the interpretation of their images of teachers and their experiences of having been taught. Lasky notes how one of the key influences on a teacher's self-concept of self as a teacher is their own experience of being taught, and says that this can help formulate their beliefs about teaching and their expectation of what it means to be a teacher (Lasky 2005). For example, Tryggvason (2009) notes the importance of getting new teachers to question their assumptions about teaching and learning in order to help them to be open to new approaches. Lasky (2005) goes on to note how early influences on teacher identity can subsequently affect how teachers deal with their contexts and react to them.

The two stories that follow are examples of how this interplay can work: in one case the interplay between context and identity appears to be working successfully and in the other it does not. This is not to suggest that one of the schools featured is somehow better than the other (although that might be the case). Both schools have found themselves responding to education policies and contexts in similar ways. The big difference between the two lies in how the two individual teachers feel about the changes that are taking place.

In previous research in this area, Bowe and Ball with Gold (1992) have outlined that teachers can use a variety of strategies – resistance, accommodation, subterfuge and conformity – when asked to respond to policy changes, and the teachers in this chapter can be seen to be using similar strategies. Indeed the narratives reveal that teachers can use a variety of resistance and compliance strategies at the same time, but directed against different policies or initiatives. The focus for this chapter is on why the teachers have responded in these particular ways.

The subject story outlined in the previous chapter is also significant here. Both of the teachers discussed herein have articulated a subject story, which is also significant in how they respond to the interplay between themselves and the contexts they are working in.

To continue with the professional compass metaphor, in this chapter we can start to see the significance of the professional compass in action. Whilst the three teachers in the previous chapter were using their subject story to explain their professional practice, here we can see that professional practice in relation to the school contexts they are working in. The values implicit in the subject story are key in how they relate and respond to the context they find themselves in. Clandinin and Connelly (1995) highlight the significance of the professional knowledge landscapes that teachers work in and in particular the 'sacred stories' that feature in them. As outlined in Chapter Two, contexts are increasingly important for teachers' professional practice, and increased prescription and accountability measures can make it more difficult for teachers to act autonomously. In fact, school contexts can be seen as significant in being influenced by teachers' identities as well as influencing them in turn. These contexts are important so that we can understand why some teachers seem to find this a challenging environment in which to work, whilst others seem to thrive within the accountability culture. To understand these differences, it is important to understand the relationship between contexts and teachers' identity, and how their identities relate to their subject stories and the extent to which they enable their professional practice to be meaningful to them.

Previous research on teachers and their work has outlined the importance of resilience and commitment in sustaining teachers through their professional careers (Day et al. 2007), but this research suggests that an important feature is how teachers feel about their work and how they are enabled to practice in line with their values and subject identity. As outlined in Chapter Two, contexts don't just shape teachers' identities but are also shaped by them. In this chapter, it is recognized that whilst the local context of the school is key in the formation and reformation of teacher identity, subject identity also provides an important benchmark of meaning for the individual teacher. This chapter explores what happens when the values of a particular school context intersect with teachers' subject identity.

An important feature of how teachers feel about their work is the extent to which their values are reflected in those of the school. Previous research has suggested that teachers can choose the extent to which they resist and comply with initiatives (Bowe and Ball with Gold 1992), but this is becoming more difficult. Departmental cultures and other networks are also significant in how teachers respond (see Puttick 2012 and Roberts 1995 for geography specific examples) but, essentially, the extent to which teachers resist and comply is a personal decision, guided by their values.

The teachers that feature in this chapter are represented here because they are two contrasting examples: one works in a context where the institutional values are closely aligned to their own, and the other works in a context where the values are quite different to their own. The cases are presented alongside each other to illuminate the complex relationship of context and identity. The examples are contrasting, but both reveal the significance of subject identity when working in a particular school context.

Mandy's subject story

Mandy was one of the first teachers to participate in this research. Although trained as a geography teacher, Mandy's preference and background is for an integrated version of the subject, combining geography with other humanities subjects. When I first interviewed her (in 1999) she was teaching in a school which matched her own values about education and the teaching of geography. The last interview with Mandy took place in 2014, when she held a post as Deputy Head in a different school, and revealed the consistency of Mandy's values and how this works in a context where she is a leader as well as a teacher.

Mandy does not necessarily self-identify as a geographer like some of the other teachers featured in this research. She is a teacher of humanities and studied for a humanities degree. Whilst her degree featured a lot of geography and her role in the first school was as head of geography, her commitment was to a curriculum which integrated geography with history and religious education. Within this context, she still had specialist geographical knowledge; indeed, her undergraduate degree focused on modules around geographical topics like environmental stewardship. She also described how much she enjoyed teaching environmental topics, particularly ones that featured the local (coastal) area. But Mandy's own interest was around issues of social justice. Mandy had also been attracted to studying theology and there is a strong theme of spirituality in her desire to teach geography: as she describes it as a subject that could inspire 'awe and wonder'.

Whilst Mandy enjoys geography ('I did find the subject fascinating and I still do'), her focus is very much on being a teacher: 'but it is more education that interests me than geography. My focus has moved into education and away from the subject.'

Mandy's school context

When I first interviewed Mandy she was teaching in a humanities faculty and, while she had responsibility for geography in the faculty, she was also Head of Humanities and had overall responsibility for the other curriculum areas. At the time of the interview, most schools in England taught history and geography as discrete subjects, sometimes combined and timetabled as humanities, but divided up into six-week blocks of history and geography. There were few schools that taught integrated humanities throughout the school curriculum, and whilst there remained a GCSE (public examination at age 16) subject of integrated humanities, the numbers studying it had dwindled. In Mandy's school, the key stage 3 (for students aged 11–14) curriculum was taught through humanities and all students took a GCSE in integrated humanities. Mandy supported this approach, as she considered it to be the most appropriate for her students, who were unlikely to proceed to study geography (or other humanities subjects) beyond secondary school. Mandy argued that the distillation of the humanities subjects, as expressed within the integrated humanities curriculum, gave students the knowledge and skills they need to operate successfully in the world.

The school Mandy taught in was a comprehensive school, situated on an estate at the edge of an English coastal town. The school's catchment area experiences significant material deprivation and this is reflected in a high number of students receiving free school meals and a high level of unauthorized absence. At the time of the interview, the school faced great challenges, and could be characterized as serving a predominantly white urban population with low levels of employment. The intake data demonstrated that these students are below the national average in attainment and above the national average in special educational needs. Mandy discussed how important it was for them to be empowered to get out of the poverty trap indicated by the school statistics.

> An absolute commitment to equality of opportunity, success and challenge for all and improving self-esteem/life chances of individuals is what I aim to achieve – empowerment of the individual through his/her educational experience.
>
> Empowerment is about strength. I do not consider the students to be victims but I do consider them to be individuals that need to be empowered through the development of particular skills, attributes, knowledge and understanding. These are of benefit to the individual, the community and society. I do believe that geography, as a discrete subject, can contribute to that.

Mandy views geography as a powerful vehicle for educational and social change, a key element in her subject story, but one she views within her commitment to a humanities-based curriculum: '[I've become more committed to integrated humanities] Because I think it is more relevant to students and I think that it is more realistic really – you don't need to make those [subject] distinctions at the lower level.'

Mandy outlined how only a few of her students went on to study the humanities subjects at a more advanced level, and those that did were able to access those courses from an integrated humanities background.

> I think that a lot of the skills they develop are related to geographical skills that are very relevant to their lives. For example, mapping skills, or graphicacy skills. I don't think that beyond that they need the intricacies of the old O level and early GCSE courses offered. I think that the decision-making activities that are required at GCSE and A level actually relate quite closely to some of the methodologies that you have in Humanities.

Her approach to teaching geography through humanities was also reflected in the approach of the school, which promoted an integrated humanities curriculum. Mandy's perspective on curriculum is reflected within this school context:

> I find it hard to fight subject corners because I really believe in kids having the opportunity to have every different kind of learning opportunity, and using every different form of thinking including aesthetic development and creative development. I'm really committed to breadth and balance.

Her attitude towards the format and composition of the school curriculum would suggest that her identity as a teacher, and her commitment to young people, is stronger than her subject identity. However, a focus on the empowerment of young people can also be seen as an extension of her subject identity, and her subject story which was orientated around social justice. These values appear to be important for Mandy, not only reflecting her perspective on geography and how it is taught, but permeating other aspects of her professional identity. Mandy has considered the needs of her students and what she can do to help them be successful. This is best exemplified in how she views her own ethnicity in relation to her students. Mandy comes from a dual heritage background and discussed how she uses this as a resource to help her students understand aspects of socialization they may not have experienced:

> I teach a lot of the Humanities course through talking about me and my family. And I talk about socialisation in terms of difference between me and my sisters and [my brother] and where my parents come from – what does it make me? And [my niece] and [my nephew] as well. What's their cultural background and what is their predominant culture? Because that is so outside the kids' experience at school.

Mandy articulates a vision of education that is closely aligned with her subject story, and what she wants her students to achieve and learn. It also fits with the structure and organization of the school. Mandy's values and those of the school appeared to be in close alignment.

Mandy in a leadership role

The last interview with Mandy took place in 2014. Since our first interview, Mandy had moved school, started a family and was working part-time but in a new role as Deputy Head. Mandy's new school had a similar student profile to her previous school. She described the catchment area as being an area of significant deprivation, and the school population had extremely high levels (over 50 per cent) of students on free school meals (an income-related measure of need). Between 40 per cent and 50 per cent of students had been identified as having special educational needs. The two major local employers had recently relocated out of the area, and Mandy described some of her students as second-generation unemployed, with little prospect or expectation of employment after leaving school. The school faced significant challenges, as many of the students were unlikely to be entered for GCSE examinations and required support to develop sufficient life skills ('such as how to use a supermarket').

In recent years, the school had experienced a lot of change, including a new school building, the loss of a sixth form, and an unfavourable Ofsted inspection report. At the time of our interview, the school was also a few months away from being turned into an academy (a new type of school, with greater autonomy and direct funding from the government). How the school has responded to these issues illustrates the ethos and values of the school and its leadership. For example, when the decision was made to close the school and reopen as an academy, it was decided to rename it to reflect a fresh start and to disassociate the school from the negative connotations of the local area. The school had also 'shopped around' for an academy sponsor. Mandy described how a list of criteria had been drawn up so that the school could select a sponsor that would support their ethos. Any religious or foreign-owned sponsors were rejected and the school searched for a sponsor that did not have a pre-determined approach to education and that was willing to work with the school to develop an approach that was suitable for the students and their particular needs. As a member of the school leadership team, Mandy would have had a significant role to play in determining and shaping this ethos, which reflects the emphasis on social justice which she had described to me several years before.

Whilst these changes appear to be line with Mandy's values, the changes that the school had been through would have been a significant challenge for her and the leadership team. Following the negative Ofsted report, the school had been allocated an advisor to help them through the transition and had been encouraged, through this process, to change aspects of school policy and practice. One of the key issues in the school, and a major theme from the Ofsted inspection, was the need to improve students' literacy. Mandy describes the focus on literacy as having had the most impact on her teaching, as all lessons must feature a literacy component. She describes how each classroom now had a 'washing line' of key words and connective words. Whilst Mandy emphasized the impact this had had on the whole school, she plays down the influence on her own teaching. She described the consistency of her own practice, how she was teaching similar lessons but had added in a literacy component. She described a lesson where the students were writing a letter to the Governor of an area in India, and how part of the lesson was used to explore how to structure and write such a letter.

One area that had been changed considerably was the structure of the curriculum, an area covered by Mandy's leadership responsibilities. In her previous school, Mandy had been a strong advocate of an integrated humanities curriculum. In her current school, they had moved away from an integrated curriculum, due, in some part, to problems in recruiting suitable teaching staff. The school still has an integrated humanities curriculum in Year 7 (aged 11–12 years), where students are taught English, history and geography in thematic blocks. Mandy described students studying a poem about the Irish potato famine in English, studying that period in history, and looking at agriculture within geography. The topics are not integrated (as was often the case in her previous school) but connected and all taught with a strong emphasis on skills. After Year 7, students were taught through the discrete subjects in Year 8 (12–13 years) and then began their chosen public examination (GCSE) subjects in Year 9 (13–14 years).

Mandy now also teaches GCSE geography, something that she enjoys. Geography remains one of the most popular option subjects in the school, and the majority of students in the school opt to study either geography or history (a reflection perhaps of the inclusion of both subjects in the English Baccalaureate (EBac) and the recently introduced progress indicators based on these EBac subjects for schools). Mandy describes how her approach to teaching geography had changed little since our first interview. She laughed as she recalled the first lessons I had observed her teach, which had been on coastal erosion in the local area, and how she was currently teaching the same topic and using many of the same approaches and strategies. Whilst the school had introduced a number of initiatives and strategies for improvement, including a good deal of monitoring, Mandy observed: 'when I close my classroom door (well, actually we aren't allowed to close our classroom doors), so when I metaphorically close my classroom door, I still teach the way I always have.'

This observation is interesting on a number of counts: Mandy is displaying a consistency in her style and approach to teaching that emphasizes the needs of her students and their particular context. Whilst the school is different, the needs of the students are similar, and Mandy's style and approach to teaching are matched accordingly. While she may no longer be teaching humanities, her commitment to social justice and empowering others is still reflected in her teaching and her work with colleagues. She describes the preferred approach of the academy sponsor as being an approach that would 'empower' the school. In addition, she discussed the impact of the monitoring strategies that the school had introduced:

as with all these things, it is really just what good teachers have always done. Good teachers know what their students should be aiming for, and they monitor and review that regularly. That is all we are asking teachers to do, we are just formalising it.

The strategies introduced by the school are similar to those in other schools in a similar situation: learning walks, a two-week marking policy regularly monitored by senior staff, and fortnightly progress checks. She outlined how all teachers had to monitor each student against their projected target on a two-weekly basis and regular meetings were held between heads of department and senior leaders where every student's progress was discussed. These strategies can be seen as part of the performativity turn within schools and could be sites of resistance. However, Mandy is able to rationalize these policy technologies as a necessary mechanism that is formalizing normal professional duties. She complies with them because they match her own values. She justified these approaches in terms of the impact they were having for individual students:

> By the end of the summer, a school should know exactly what its results will be [in the public examinations] . . . we know what all the kids are doing so we can target which ones we have the potential to make a difference with, and which are doing fine.

Increased accountability, pressures from Ofsted and a shift to academy status are all trends that have affected Mandy's context. Her school, driven partly by her own leadership, has responded in similar ways to other schools: requiring regular monitoring and surveillance of teachers and being more prescriptive in classroom-based activities. However, Mandy makes sense of these changes in the way that she has always made sense of the classroom – by focussing on how the changes can empower her students. The alignment of her own values with those of the school means she feels able to teach in a way that she is committed to. The aspects of her subject identity that were meaningful for her in her earlier school are still powerful drivers in her current role. She has had to make changes and compromises, but she can see the benefits for the students and can rationalize these changes as not having a huge impact on her practice because she can interpret them as improving students' life chances and social situations. Her only concession was that teaching was 'less fun, less enjoyable' than she had previously found it. Mandy's story reveals the remarkable consistency in her professional values, driven by a need to do well for her students, and a sense of social justice as it applies to geography and to teaching.

A contrasting case

Mandy's narratives reveal a consistent set of values that have sustained her through her career and changing school circumstances. Her values appear to be aligned with the schools' contexts and cultures. In the narrative that follows, Daisy tells a different story about how her experience of adapting to school cultures and influences has brought her practice into conflict with her subject identity. Her school's culture has significantly challenged her subject identity and professional values.

Daisy had been teaching for eight years, both in England and abroad. She had studied for her Masters degree and, due to her studies, had worked in a range of part-time and full-time positions both in London and in the north of England, both to fund and complement her studies. In her interview, Daisy contrasted working in two particular schools, both in London, which had given her different teaching experiences. At this time, Daisy had just left the second of these schools to take up a new position. These two schools make up the main contexts referred to here.

My relationship with Daisy started when she began her Masters degree, for which I was her tutor. After completing her Masters degree, Daisy took a teaching post in Asia and we kept in touch. It was during her time in Asia that she decided to undertake further research and so our professional dialogue and relationship continued subsequent to her return. It was on the basis of our discussions during this five year period, and having seen Daisy work in school contexts where she had been happy, and then subsequently unhappy, that I asked her to participate in this study.

This background is significant because at the time of the interviews, Daisy was an experienced teacher, having worked in a variety of different contexts and roles. Daisy was (and is) firmly committed to engaging in practitioner research, and had undertaken further qualifications at her own expense. Like the other teachers in this research, she is a deeply reflective, articulate and committed geography teacher, who was also desperately unhappy: and I wanted to find out why.

Daisy's narrative reveals a conflict between the school culture and her own subject story. This conflict became amplified as she contrasted the working practices of these schools with previous school contexts where she had felt happy and fulfilled. Whilst Daisy blamed the managerial style and approaches of these schools, her narrative also reveals that the context and recent histories of the school are influential in shaping the school culture and the professional expectations for teachers within the school. In order to understand the conflict Daisy experienced, it is useful to start with her subject story.

Daisy's subject story

Growing up in a rural part of England, Daisy describes herself as being a bit of a rebel when she was a pupil. She describes her parents, and the village they lived in, as being quite conservative, but also says that she was given a lot of opportunity for self-expression. Her desire was initially to study anthropology, but her parents encouraged her to study a more traditional subject and so she chose geography. This appeared to be a good choice for Daisy as she was interested in the subject and describes an inspirational secondary school geography teacher, who had travelled widely and used his vast collection of photographs and slides as a key resource in his classroom. Daisy felt the draw of the 'exotic' and became fascinated with places. She still describes herself as having 'itchy feet' and travels extensively during her vacation time. At university,

Daisy became attracted to aspects of cultural geography, a category of geography that focuses on people and their activities. The study of cultural geography enabled Daisy to combine these interests and to understand something that, for her, was 'real':

> I used to skateboard a lot and I was really interested in how young people use space and place. It was frowned upon quite negatively. There was a lot of anti-skateboarding campaigns. I used to wear a hood and ripped jeans and I liked skateboarding around and when the cultural geographers started talking about that I was like "oh you are actually talking about things that are real" and it was far more real to me.

She also explains how the study of the real has been an enduring interest for her: 'The exotic is just how different people live, isn't it? And how different people relate to where they live. I'm fascinated by people and how they understand where they live and how they relate and imagine their worlds.'

These interests were reflected in her own research work. Her undergraduate dissertation was on how young people and their places were portrayed in the media, a theme that she returned to in her Masters dissertation and further research.

This ongoing interest in people and how they understand their places is strongly reflected in her approach to teaching and learning. Daisy's practice as a geography teacher is characterized by using a lot of 'hands on' and 'outdoor' activities. In the school where Daisy was the happiest, she describes how her practice reflected these approaches:

> In [the school] we went on loads [of field trips] or even if they wouldn't let you take Year Seven out, we would go around the school and map crime or get them doing bits and bobs around the school.

> When I was in the school in South London there were people there who are really interested in the subject and they spent quite a lot of time developing really exciting resources and everyone was kind of pro-geography . . . The head would let me invite in town planners, would let me have time off time-table to do a version of [a simulation game]. He [the Head] was very open to you doing experiential learning, or taking them down the road and looking at places, and talking about where they felt safe or unsafe, and going around the school, doing little mini field trips and things like that.

Daisy's description of the kind of teaching she likes to do reveals her values about geography and her approach to teaching geography. Whilst she described a range of teaching approaches, her preference is for activities that focus on 'real' geography, experienced through engagement with the real world and through investigation. She promotes active and field-based approaches to learning. In the school that Daisy describes above she was able to teach in alignment with her values and this is where she reported being happiest.

Daisy left her position at this school as she felt that she needed to take on a subject leadership role, and it was in her next school that she found that her approach to teaching geography came into sharp contrast with the approach of the school.

Working in a difficult environment

The school that Daisy moved to was in a similar area of London. However, the approach to teaching and learning in the school and the management style were both very different. In terms of teaching and learning, the second school was far more prescriptive:

> It was also quite a dictatorial environment . . . everything had to be structured in a certain way – to the point where PowerPoints had to be a certain colour and text boxes had to be a certain colour within that. And it was a bit much for me I think.

The degree of prescription was reflected not just in the presentation of instructional materials but also in the types of images and resources that Daisy was encouraged to use. She felt that any activities where students were out of their seats would not be acceptable:

> I thought that you would be looked at if you had children standing up in the classroom even if they were going around and getting information from different places and some of them [the school leadership] would be looking in to see if you are doing something that [they did not like].

This degree of prescription in how lessons were to be conducted had a huge impact on her teaching of geography. In particular, Daisy was concerned about the monitoring of images being used in lessons. Daisy had recently read Paul Gilroy's book *There Ain't No Black in the Union Jack* (1987), and had wanted to discuss with her students how they felt about some of the issues raised:

> I remember we did a few lessons [in her previous school] on settlement migration and multicultural Britain and I developed it with a colleague. He did stuff on racism in football and I did stuff on Rock Against Racism. But in this [her new] school I think if you even mentioned colour or you even mentioned ethnicity or religion or anything like that, it would have been extremely frowned upon because you were mentioning the something that could be contrived in different ways. It was bonkers . . . as you were not able to engage in dialogue about political things with the young people. For example [the head] walked in on a new teacher who was using a picture of a child starving in an African country and [the Head] just said it wasn't allowed . . . "you can't show that image". I know that the history teacher was told off for showing a picture of lynching when talking about the effects of

slavery. If you were teaching development, you were only allowed to show positive images. You are aware of things when you are teaching, especially in London which is a very multicultural place, and you would never just show one place as being just one thing. But you're aware of that as a professional.

The level of interference by the school leadership was having a direct impact on Daisy's practice. She reported how she had to reconsider both the content of the curriculum, and how to present it to students. In addition, Daisy described organizing a number of fieldtrips that the school had later cancelled, and the impact this had had on her:

> I probably have stopped doing things in retrospect . . . [field trips she tried to organize] just never ended up happening and I felt like I was spending a lot of my time doing things that would just get cancelled. When it happens once you are fine. But when it happens consistently you feel beaten down by it.

Even though Daisy was the Head of Geography, a senior leader who also taught geography exerted a lot of control over which case studies could be used in lessons. Daisy described trying to change the case studies being used for GCSE geography and her reasons for doing so:

> Sometimes case studies in the textbook are really useful and relevant but sometimes the case study in the textbook is from 1986! And there is something in the news, something that the children are going to be aware of and going to be talking about with their families that is more relevant. Also nowadays with Twitter and with news websites, you can get so much information, so many amazing graphics, and video so quickly, that in a way some of the things that you can make are probably better than what is in the textbook.

Her attempts to change and update the geography curriculum had been blocked by the assistant head who had refused to teach new case studies. She contrasted this approach with the one she had experienced in her previous school where she was able to introduce new units that were in line with her values about the subject:

> You could do a lot of cultural geography and we would talk about how places were constructed. And we did really fun things such as developing a sense of place of Margate using Chas & Dave. It would be far more kind of fun I guess.

On one hand, Daisy could rationalize the approach as being a result of the school's 'history of having poor results'. She also likened what was happening in the school as being driven by the school seeking to adapt to the Ofsted agenda and trying to find ways to support a fast-changing and inexperienced teaching staff:

It felt that I had to teach to a specific formula that fitted OFSTED. I understand why it had to be done that way because the school has got a lot of problems. It has got a really high staff turnover and so it needs resources to be left in place. There are a lot of young teachers in there and probably young teachers do need that kind of structure but it didn't really suit me.

For Daisy, the prescriptive school approach meant that she could not use the range of outside speakers, creative teaching and learning strategies that she felt was important to learning geography. In addition, the high level of control and prescription over teaching in the school was accompanied by a management style that she found difficult. She contrasted her experience in her previous school where she felt more valued as a professional:

You felt that you were known by them [the leadership team] and they would be able to have a conversation with you. If there was a problem you would be asked 'what about this?' and it would be sorted out quite quickly. You'd be told informally and everything wasn't a big drama.

In her recent school, teachers were required to account for their time in a much more prescriptive way. A key focus of this level of interference was described by Daisy in the focus on marking. Whilst she had been able 'mark things properly' in her previous school, this had been as a result of a school-wide discussion about better assessment practices:

So they were quite open, but when they would bring in new policies they would give you examples of marking and get you to discuss it in a far more open way. It would mean a lot of sharing and it would be far more open.

In her subsequent school, not only were the marking practices more rigidly prescriptive but the monitoring was more bureaucratic: 'you were told two days before there was a review of all the [student] books you've ever looked at.'

Daisy was also concerned that this approach had had a negative impact on the school staff generally:

You didn't know where you stood there because there would be all these rash decisions that would come out from nowhere. There would be no follow-up. But I think there was quite a culture of unhappiness amongst the staff there as well. So I felt that every week I was dealing with somebody who was in tears and I think if people are miserable then everyone starts moaning, and it becomes a moaning place.

Clearly the school culture and context was having an effect on Daisy, but the worst thing for her was the level of curriculum control. Daisy was not allowed to teach young people's geographies, an area of interest to Daisy. She felt that she was unable to resist or contest the dominant approach of the school, because of how their judgements about her could affect her career:

> At the end of the day, you've got to get a reference from the people you work for. There is also pay involved as well. You want to get through the threshold[1] and you don't want your work to be a battleground. I don't want to go to work everyday and to be fighting with my managers. There's no point.

Daisy also pointed out that 'falling out with your managers' had an effect on her sense of professionalism:

> But I guess one of the biggest problems I find with teaching is that sometimes you do feel like you're on repeat. It is the lack of voice within the teaching profession that winds me up . . . you don't feel very listened to . . . in general, in terms of policy, as a teacher you need to be listened to.

She describes getting to the point where she felt that teaching was pointless: 'just like digging holes', as this lack of voice empties out the meaning of teaching for her.

> It's just doing as you are told and who says that the person who is telling you is right? You need to have your eyes open to a different way of looking at things and to listen to different voices about things.

Daisy's subject identity, the focus on understanding the 'real' through experiential and discovery learning, reflects her values about teaching geography. Daisy wants to empower her students so that they can explore their own opinions. However, working in a context that tries to control and limit Daisy's professional autonomy causes her to question the very nature of her work and its professional value. The frustration that Daisy articulates has led her to question her future in teaching.

Daisy's sense of a declining professionalism got even worse. In a further conversation, she recalled a conversation she had with her new line-manager (a Head of Humanities) after the school had been inspected by Ofsted. During the post-inspection party, the Head of Humanities told Daisy about a new book she had read called *The Lazy Teacher's Guide to Teaching*. The Head of Humanities had been so excited by this book that she was determined to make it the key focus of future developments in the department. Daisy had responded positively but had pointed out that 'we need to critique things as well, it can't all be about just one book.' Daisy relayed this anecdote to me as a precursor to her explaining why she had started to question whether to stay in teaching. These two experiences had led her to conclude that teaching was being reduced to being 'obsessed with showing progress', and as a result this was 'taking away the enjoyment of learning'. She described a climate of fear 'where people are scared for their jobs', and where the price of not conforming to a reform agenda was extremely high.

She described how it made her feel: 'I just felt miserable so I'm leaving. I was totally miserable. I was working 70 hours a week. I was so miserable and I thought: I'm not doing this any longer.'

Subject identity and the professional context

Daisy's account of her 'battle' with the school shows how intensely emotional and draining it can be when the school's values and those of the teacher are not in alignment. Daisy has a strong sense of the power, draw and purpose of geography for young people, which had great meaning for her. The school context, however, appears to have eroded away her opportunity to teach in line with her professional and subject values. She described how she had started resisting these pressures but found herself starting to take on the dominant culture of the school: 'I think you learn what people want to see. You want to please your manager and you want to please people you work for. And so you teach in that style a little bit more.'

The dominant approach of the school was intended to support the teachers in raising results and achieving a good inspection outcome. However, the ways in which this was being accomplished were seen as a direct threat to Daisy in a number of ways, limiting her professional choices about what to teach and how to teach. Daisy also wanted to improve the school's results and for it to achieve a good inspection outcome, but she disagreed with the school on how this could be brought about.

The level of school intervention had a direct impact on the content of the geography curriculum and the approaches to teaching and learning geography, including which knowledges were acceptable to be featured in classroom. The preferred school approaches around the use of textbooks and enforced revision clubs were given much higher status in the school than the active and participatory learning approaches preferred by Daisy. These alternative approaches were so removed from Daisy's professional and subject values that they were emptied out of meaning and purpose. For her this approach represented an anti-educational approach to teaching geography. The dominant pedagogical approach of the school created barriers for her, preventing her from teaching in a way that she considered to be the best for her students to learn geography.

Daisy's resistance was very difficult for her emotionally. She described 'loving teaching' and 'loving her students', but the difference between the school approach and her own preferred approach was too much to bear, and she had started to reconsider her career in teaching geography.

It is difficult to overstate how closely aligned Daisy's motivations to teach geography are with her subject identity. For her, the very purpose of geography is about learning something 'real'. (Her practice did have other more traditional elements of geography teaching.) This stands in contrast to the preferred approach of the school on using tried and tested case study resources. For Daisy the construction of geography is at the nexus of experience and everyday life with geographical concepts that help explain that experience. The construction of a school geography from out-of-date case studies and textbooks goes against her sense of 'lived' and child-centred geography, her professional and subject identity and values.

What is different and noteworthy about this case is that, for Daisy, the compromises are too much: the difference between how she wants to teach and how she is expected to teach is too great to be bridged through compromise but requires her to undertake a wholescale re-evaluation of her life as a teacher.

Context and identity

In this chapter I have outlined two contrasting experiences; however, this is not to suggest that all teachers work in one or other of these extremes. The distinction is made to highlight the contrast between working in a school setting that is in line with a teacher's own values and beliefs and working in a school where the aims, purposes and values of education are drastically different. Daisy's narrative reveals that it is not just an issue of values alignment, but also one of the extent to which the school's values are prescribed and the degree of agency and professional autonomy teachers feel they are allowed.

Mandy's school also had school-wide policies regarding curriculum, accountability and teachers' practice (including the need to focus on literacy in every lesson). For Mandy this degree of interference was not a problem as the changes were in line with her own professional values. For both Mandy and Daisy, their professional values appear to be closely aligned with their subject identity, as expressed through their subject stories. Mandy's subject identity is grounded in values around social justice and empowerment. Daisy's values are more focused on exploring and understanding the real. Each of these approaches stems from how they identify with the subject and what it means to them as learners and teachers, and is consistent with why they think the subject is important. These values about learning also appear to stem from their subject identity.

The intention in highlighting this relationship is not to suggest that one approach is 'right' or another 'wrong' but to show the emotional impact it can have for teachers and their work: the significance of the interplay between context and identity. For both teachers featured in this chapter, the nexus is sharply (but not only) felt in the school context. For Mandy, her approach to teaching and learning, and the style of curriculum she preferred, were the advocated approach of the school and so she was able to teach in the way that she thought was best, making only minor modifications to her practice. For Daisy, the tension appeared to be keenly felt at the site of the classroom, in terms of how she was able to teach, what content she was expected to cover, and even down to the style of her teaching resources. For Daisy, this level of prescription and control represented a threat to her professional practice, as she felt her day-to-day decision making was being taken away from her. Mandy did not discuss being 'controlled' or having to adhere to levels of prescription, perhaps because she agreed with school policies and did not see them as detracting from her own sense of professionalism. The common factor does not appear to be the level of prescription in school policies but the extent to which the individual teachers saw them as being aligned with their own priorities and perspectives.

In these two school cultures values are expressed in a variety of ways including:

- Expectations about classroom behaviours.
- Classroom resources and their use.
- The school organization: the place of geography as a school subject.
- The school curriculum: how geography is defined and shaped within the school curriculum.
- The dominant pedagogical approaches promoted and preferred by the school.
- The assessment and examination options offered by the school.

Each of these elements can have a direct impact on the teacher's individual practice. Combined they articulate the status and value of individual subjects and the autonomy of particular teachers. For an individual, the significance of this will depend on the extent to which their values are aligned with those being expressed through the school culture.

In the cases of both Mandy and Daisy presented here, the context of the school culture is key. Both of them describe working in schools in challenging circumstances. In Mandy's first school the challenge was to support students to achieve their best. For Daisy's school the challenge was to teach in a certain way and to get a good inspection result. Both sacred stories are about achievement and success, but the interpretation of 'success' is different. This is not to suggest that one approach is inherently 'better' than the other but that the intentions of educational institutions reflect what they perceive education to be for. These purposes and aims are embodied through various mechanisms (structural and procedural) within the school. These can be seen as articulations of the school culture. The expression of that culture is in how schools communicate their expectations to teachers.

The two accounts also illustrate the emotional intensity of operating in different school cultures. Mandy's accounts are full of optimism and positivity. Daisy describes herself as miserable. Research on teacher identity emphasizes the importance of teachers' emotions and highlights the extent to which their identity can be an enabling aspect of professional practice (Hargreaves 2001). This is emotional precisely because these emotions are so embedded within a teacher's individual identity and how that is recognized by the school culture.

Daisy's narrative is one that greatly concerns me. Daisy has worked in a number of schools, and in her most recent employments has found it difficult to reconcile her own ideas about teaching geography with the values and practices required by the institution. In her discussions with me, Daisy bemoans 'education today' and has expressed concern that there are no schools left that will enable her to teach in the way that she wishes to. Daisy has had experience of teaching in a school which she felt shared her values, but her inability to find another context that shares these values has led her to conclude that there are no longer suitable environments for her to work in. Daisy's narrative poses some important questions about how individual teachers with strong professional values and identities are able to work productively in the current climate of education.

The attitudes towards teaching expressed by these teachers are deeply rooted in their sense of what it means to be a teacher of their subject. Their values and beliefs are grounded in their subject identity, which appears to be a strong driver for their sustained motivation and for their practice. This analysis goes beyond structural or sociological approaches that define teacher identity and professionalism in terms of structure and agency. Their understanding of teaching and learning is connected to their engagement with the subject – what it means to them. As with the other cases in this research, the connection appears to begin when learning becomes an important part of the personal narrative and, as such, is a focal reflection point for the decision to teach (and the desire to remain in teaching). For Mandy the motivation to learn more about the world is connected to her sense of the liberation around education. For Daisy, the school's approach to education denies her students access to the outside world, the thing that she thinks they should be investigating. It is not that these schools are overly prescriptive, or indeed not prescriptive enough. It is that their approach to teaching and learning can complement or challenge the teacher's image of what it means to be a teacher of their subject.

The professional knowledge landscapes outlined in this chapter have been significant influences on the two teachers featured. The focus on how these landscapes interplay with the teacher's own professional compass goes some way to revealing why teachers respond the way they do to education reform. It also goes some way to explaining the 'persistent grammar of schooling' articulated by Tyack and Cuban (1995). If teachers with significantly different values find it emotionally difficult to stay in a particular school context, then it seems logical to suggest that those who stay have a vested interest in maintaining certain value positions which they share with the school. This makes long-lasting change unlikely, unless that change is formulated within a shared set of values. This can be observed when new school leadership tries to dramatically change the culture of a school, often with devastating results.

Note

1 Threshold was an additional payment for experienced teachers who met certain requirements.

7

NAVIGATING CLASSROOM PRACTICE

In the previous chapters we have seen how teachers' values, as expressed through a subject story, can influence their practice at a personal level and also within their school context. One of the arguments discussed in Chapter One was how teachers' subject knowledge can affect pupils' achievement. Whilst it was acknowledged that what you know is important up to a point, it is how teachers use that subject knowledge that appears to be key beyond that. So far we have seen how having a subject story, or values that stem from subject expertise, can be important for teachers' identities and how they relate to their contexts. However, the next step is to explore how that can affect their classroom practice.

Researching classroom practice is difficult. Individual lessons may not be indicative of practice over time, and teachers can react differently with some classes compared to others. However, when looking at classroom practice it is possible to get a sense of teachers' values 'in action' – how their values can have an effect on their decision making both in the enactment of the curriculum and in the 'hot action' (Schon 1987) of the classroom.

Classrooms are complex and busy places and it is difficult to attribute classroom action to particular thoughts, ideas or practices. Therefore, when considering what goes on inside a classroom, it is important to consider how it fits within the school culture itself, how the teacher relates to that school culture and the teacher's own background and identity. This chapter therefore focuses on just one teacher, albeit a rather interesting and unusual case.

As outlined in the previous chapter, the professional compass metaphor can help to reveal how teachers respond to different contexts, the professional knowledge landscape. This also holds true in this chapter. The professional compass here is particularly focused on classroom practice. There are many influences on a teacher's professional practice, including school policies about preferred pedagogies and pressures from inspection regimes (official discourses). However, as Bowe and Ball with Gold (1992) have highlighted, the implementation of these policies requires interpretation by individual teachers and this is influenced by the school contexts and other cultural groups that the teacher may belong to. This is also true of classroom practice, which is idiosyncratic to individual teachers. This chapter argues that the subject-based values – the subject story and the values that underpin it – can also be influential on teachers' classroom practice.

Classroom practice

The particular values perspective of the school and whether it aligns with a teacher's own values can determine whether a teacher feels able to resist or comply with the dominant culture of the school. For some schools the trend has been to be more and more prescriptive in directing and controlling the work of teachers. This can be seen through a range of school policies and has been identified by Ball, Maguire and Braun (2012).

However the classroom context is to some extent more private for teachers as, when the classroom door is closed, teachers are more in control of the moment to moment interactions. Indeed the curriculum making model explored in Chapter Three, places the emphasis on individual teachers to take control of their curriculum making in their particular classrooms.

Both of the teachers featured in Chapter Six described how their subject identity was having an impact on their work in schools. In both cases there were indications of how this can have an impact on classroom practice. For example, Mandy described how even changes in the school's emphasis on literacy had not made her change her practice dramatically. For Daisy, the ways that the school were requiring her to teach were too much for her to bear. However, these are two extremes and, for most teachers, there is a swaying between resistance and compliance as observed by Bowe and Ball with Gold (1992). In this chapter, I suggest that this swaying between resistance and compliance happens within the hot action of the classroom. How teachers decide to behave and whether to comply or not with school policies will be influenced by their subject identity.

Andrew is the focus of this chapter because many of the professional knowledge dilemmas faced by teachers can be seen in this one particular example, which makes it a useful illustration of the effect of subject identity on professional practice. As with the other teachers who participated in this study, Andrew's narrative reveals that his current contexts are creating specific dilemmas that are particularly influential on his classroom practice. These dilemmas directly affect how the subject can be presented, used and developed in the classroom. The lesson recounted here, and Andrew's accompanying discussion of it, shows how these dilemmas are played out in the use of his subject expertise and how he skilfully handles different knowledges. Andrew oscillates between compliance and resistance. His judgement reflects his subject identity and subject story and how these can influence classroom level practice.

In Chapter Three it was argued that there is a consensus within geography education about the role of the teacher as a curriculum maker. The curriculum making model (see Figure 3.1) is used to illustrate the three sources of energy that teachers need to keep in balance. The emphasis is placed on the teacher, as the curriculum maker, not to allow undue dominance of any of the three areas. The reality of teachers' work is that influences from the education or school culture can often exert a strong influence in the classroom, limiting teachers' opportunities to maintain this balance. The narrative featured in this chapter reveals how Andrew achieves this balance through nuanced judgement, guided by his subject identity.

To explore Andrew's situation, this chapter will first outline the school and education contexts that he is working in, and how they have recently changed. These are particularly significant for Andrew because he works in the school where he was a pupil; therefore changes in the school culture challenge his experiences as a pupil in the school. In his lessons Andrew handles these knowledge dilemmas through his classroom practice. His discussion of his teaching reveals the compromises he makes, whilst developing, reframing and adjusting his own sense of professional practice.

Changing school culture

As a former pupil, Andrew joined the school as a teacher with a lot of prior knowledge of the school culture, the local community, and the dominant approaches to teaching and learning. In the last five years, the school had undergone significant changes, particularly in the accepted approaches to teaching and learning, changes which reflect the policy and education shifts discussed in Chapter Two. Andrew described how he perceived this transition. Whilst the factual details of the transition have been verified for accuracy, the account reflects how Andrew feels about how these changes have been implemented.

The school had been a local grammar school for boys. It became an academy in the last three years. In a region dominated by grammar schools, the school was seen as successful and was known for good results. The school was regarded as fairly 'traditional', something which Andrew considers to be tied into its grammar school identity. However, this grammar school identity was in the process of change as the school became a 'new' academy, a transition that has meant the school needed to adapt its shared understanding of what was 'good' pedagogy, teaching and learning.

The transition from a grammar school into an academy has resulted in a great deal of conflict and change. The transition was overseen by a new Headteacher who, in turn, brought together a new senior leadership team. The changes have meant high staff-turnover and a range of initiatives to 'modernise' the teaching within the school. All of this occurred against a backdrop of an Ofsted inspection, preceded by a 'mock' inspection. It was recognized that the school, whilst previously known for its good results, had not improved these results year on year, and as such was seen by the new leadership team as complacent. The focus of the criticism was on classroom practice, which was perceived as being too much like a 'grammar school' – traditional and didactic. In preparation for the Ofsted visit, the school focused on changing classroom practice, influenced by a series of recommendations from a team which conducted a mock-Ofsted pre-inspection in the school.

The extent of the changes happening in the school culture at this time can be observed as happening at two levels: one at the level of the school, its organization and administration, and the second at the classroom level, what the school expected of its teachers in terms of teaching and learning. Although the focus of this chapter is on the classroom, the backdrop of the school-level changes and the influence these had on the Department reveals the changing school culture, the impact of the education context and how these cultural influences affected Andrew's practice.

First, it is important to outline the political and social backdrop of a transition from a grammar school to an academy. There have been two waves of academy developments. Under the UK New Labour government, academies were introduced as a way of 'turning around' failing schools. Schools that were deemed to be failing were closed and reopened with a new name, academy status, and sometimes with a new management team and private partners. The subsequent Coalition government extended this scheme to any school that was deemed 'outstanding' by Ofsted and the second wave of academies were significantly different. Already successful schools, 'new' academies were able to be more autonomous in their management and funding.

In Andrew's school, the local context is significant. In an area that still uses the 11-Plus examination to determine which secondary schools young people attend, the competition for places in good local schools is high. The area has a number of grammar or selective entry schools (there are six grammar schools within a 3 mile radius), and a range of non-selective schools, which serve the students who are not able to get places in grammar schools. Under such a system, local competition is fierce and a school's reputation (and in particular how it compares to other schools in the area) is an important factor in attracting the best students. The top schools are able to attract the most able students. For a school in this situation, the transition to academy status would provide additional autonomy, and might increase its competitiveness. For a school like Andrew's it was also seen as an opportunity to modernize, and to update a traditional and outdated curriculum.

The leadership team instigated the transition to academy status and, whilst the changes to the practice of the school appeared minimal at first, it was in the light of the new academy's first Ofsted that change really started to appear. The first Ofsted inspection for a school that has undergone such a change is significant, as the first inspection judgement is widely regarded as a benchmark of the success of the new school. Andrew reports that the senior leadership team was clearly concerned about the impending Ofsted inspection, which was operating under a new (and widely determined to be tougher) framework for inspection. The new Head (who had come from a comprehensive school background) was concerned that the grammar school approach to teaching and learning would not fit well in the Ofsted framework and so sought to change the teaching and learning culture of the school.

The senior leadership team contracted a team to conduct a mock inspection that would highlight the areas of the school that needed to change. The effects of this mock inspection caused shock waves throughout the school. Andrew describes the experience:

> [The Head] hired this OFSTED company to come in and they absolutely slated the school. The report was circulated and it was just so disheartening. They said that the only reason that our school gets good results was because the kids are self-motivated. The teaching was awful. Everything negative that could be said, they said.
>
> I think it was a completely unfair assessment. But I think a lot of the teachers who had been here a long time took it very personally and so that's why morale in the school just went down after that.

The criticisms that emerged from the mock Ofsted inspection appeared to be directly focused on the teaching and learning approaches in the school:

> Two of the teachers got criticised because they were standing at the front, but these people walked into the lesson literally for two minutes and then walked out again and so if you were spotted talking at that moment, then you were criticised.

The critical attention given to teaching-from-the-front was described by Andrew as an attack on what was seen as the dominant approach of teaching and learning in the school. As a former grammar school, so-called 'traditional' approaches (such as direct instruction) to teaching and learning were common-place. Critical accounts of Ofsted have noted their aversion to this style of teaching (Christodoulou 2014; Peal 2014). The mock-inspection team was also critical of more traditional approaches to teaching: 'I think they came in with this sort of like comprehensive [school] hat on and couldn't really relate to some of what they were seeing.'

These criticisms seemed to attack the very core of the school culture and sent the school into a tailspin of reform and change focused directly on modernizing classroom practice.

> I think that really put off people from being able to teach well in some ways, because they were so concerned with their lesson: are my learning objectives on the board? Have I got a starter written on the board? I think you just end up losing sight of the subject because you are so concerned with the singing and dancing and all those other things.

Following the mock inspection, the school laid on a range of in-service training days, followed by a system of in-house inspections to closely monitor individual teachers' practices. In Andrew's account he describes the training provided as coming from an 'outsider' perspective, a perspective that did not understand the culture of the school: 'We've had lots of external people come in to deliver insets (in-service training) who are saying "you have to do it like this" and there are people at this school, who are thinking "I'm not going to do that".'

The challenges from the mock inspection appeared to get at the very heart of what had been the old grammar school culture. There are clearly a number of factors that have been influential in this changing of the school culture. First, the new Head appeared to be at loggerheads with most of the staff and his vision for the school seemed to be in opposition to the dominant school culture. Secondly the mechanisms used by the senior leadership team were seen as an affront to the professional autonomy of the staff. Andrew acknowledges that something in the school needed to change: 'I think that the standards have dropped in the last 10 years probably. I think the standards of teaching were higher when I was at the school than they are now.'

However, Andrew attributes the decline in teaching standards not to complacency by the staff, but to the enforced changes in how good teaching is defined. I asked him why standards had declined and he responded: 'because of the changes in teaching methods in some ways.' I queried then why the initiatives that had been brought in to make the teaching better had actually made them worse. Andrew offered an example of how the development and introduction of a prescriptive marking policy had changed the nature of how marking and feedback was undertaken in the school.

> People who work at [this school] have always loved their job and one of the reasons why I stayed in contact with some of my teachers was because they put their heart and soul into the job. So I would do extra essays because I wanted to do well, and they would mark them in their spare time. But I think now people are becoming quite resentful towards giving things out of the goodness of their heart, because of all the things that are being imposed on them. I think it's like a lack of respect to the profession, to your professionalism.

Throughout his interview, Andrew frequently referred back to his experience as a pupil at the school, and used this positive experience to illustrate the damage the changes were doing.

Andrew's subject story

The start of Andrew's subject story begins when he was a pupil at the school. His primary school education did not feature geography to a great extent. He recognizes that, as one of the first group of students affected by the Literacy and Numeracy Strategies,[1] he did not receive much geographical education until he attended secondary school. It was at secondary school that his experience of learning geography was transformed, which he attributes to the three geography teachers who worked at the school (and who were still working there when he joined as a teacher). Although, in his interview, Andrew referred to these three teachers by their first names, he described the practice of the three teachers as indistinguishable, always referring to their teaching and approach to teaching as being consistent across the three. For Andrew, these three teachers were traditional, didactic and 'grammar school' in their approach, often standing at the front of the class and lecturing to the students, requiring the students in turn to take extensive notes. Whilst Andrew recounts that this might not sound very exciting, his experience of learning in this way was extremely fulfilling, because the teachers presented geography in exciting and interesting ways. The teachers enjoyed sharing their extensive geographical knowledge with students and were engaging to interact with. Andrew described how their lessons seemed to fly by, and how the teachers developed personal relationships with their students and encouraged them to complete extra work. Andrew acknowledges that their range of teaching and learning strategies was limited, but as a student he still found their lessons engaging, exciting and rewarding.

This experience had a powerful effect on Andrew's understanding of geography and his beliefs about teaching and learning geography. His conceptions of geography teachers were that they should have extensive subject knowledge, so that they could converse on a wide range of subjects, and for Andrew this appeared to be tied in to the grammar school approach, a strong feature of the school and one that he contrasts with an alternative, or 'comprehensive' approach.

Andrew joined the school as a teacher just as his former geography teachers were approaching retirement. At the time of interview, all three of the teachers had retired and the department had been replenished with new staff. The three original teachers were known for their outstanding results, particularly at A level, another factor that Andrew attributes to their excellent subject knowledge. However, the last few years of their practice, as the school was entering its transition period, were difficult for them:

> They went from having all outstanding lessons like 10 or 20 years ago, to the last 5 years never going higher than a [grade] 'two' (or Good) because the line manager and senior leadership said 'no you are talking too much'. They had to change their methods.

Andrew does not describe the teachers as being resistant to change. In fact, when he started working at the school, he felt that they were keen to learn from him:

> In a way they learnt a lot from me in the few years we worked together . . . I had new ideas which they took on board, unlike when [the new Head of Department] came in, and tried to impose his ways on them. We learnt together so I would show them things and they would say "that's a good idea" and use them themselves.

The introduction of a new Head of Department, who tried to micro-manage the teachers, reinforced the new approaches being encouraged by the school:

[The new Head of Department] was very good at micromanaging: when I came into the Department there were PowerPoints with reams and reams and reams of complex information that you shouldn't really be showing kids, because they can't really take that much information in. I think there was a lot of standing at the front and teachers talking about the subject and the students writing it down. Obviously they were getting the outcomes because the kids are motivated. They are engaged and they want to learn, and they would go away and learn it. And [the new Head of Department] came in and was 'obviously you can't teach like that. There has to be a mystery. There has to be this, and this and this'. But equally I don't think he had the balance because I don't think he had the depth of knowledge. So he really skimmed through things. He would get very angry when the other teachers had spent too long on one topic because he was saying 'you've got to get through it, you've got to get through it' and I think the depth was lost.

Andrew's account of the two contrasting positions is revealing about his own subject story. Having been a product of the more traditional approach, Andrew appreciates the importance of detailed subject knowledge. Similarly, his teaching practice experience was in a range of inner-city comprehensives and there he learnt a range of teaching and learning strategies and came to appreciate their value in helping students learn. However, he characterizes the approach of the new Head of Department, as representing the 'new' approach of the school as 'micro-managing' and using strategies without a sense of rationale or purpose and contrasts this with the overly detailed approach of the traditional teachers. He is critical but also sees the value in both approaches.

His subject story is more related to the teaching of geography than to geography as a subject or discipline. Whilst he claims he 'loves' geography, Andrew found it difficult to describe himself as a geographer. At school he had been successful at geography and enjoyed some of the extra challenges he was given as an advanced student. He found his first year at university challenging, but enjoyed subsequent studies when he was able to specialize. His degree content reflects an interest in a political dimension in geography, including radical and development studies, and this continues in his current preference for A level when teaching topics based on conflicts and challenges. He describes himself as being:

a human geographer because I think my interests lie more within the urban world than the rural world. I am more interested in people and interactions with people and their spaces rather than geomorphological processes because I just think that's a bit more dull. I'm interested more in contemporary issues. We've been looking at contemporary conflict and challenges at A2 and in globalisation. How the world is evolving and changing, rather than how it was formed in the first place.

Andrew sees school geography as playing an important role in helping young people understand the changing world.

The idea that dominates Andrew's view of geography is what it means to learn the subject. His subject story is full of references to being a learner of the subject at this school, and to his images of what geography is like to learn, dominated by his own experience. This places his subject story in conflict with the changing school culture. How Andrew deals with this conflict can be seen in his classroom practice.

Andrew's classroom practice

The tensions between Andrew's subject story and the school culture are not immediately obvious in his classroom practice: Andrew is a skilled and accomplished teacher. However, he shows evidence of compliance and resistance. What is interesting is when he decides to comply and when he chooses to resist. For Andrew, the act of resistance comes with concerns about his practice being judged, graded and perceived as ineffectual. Similarly, the act of compliance brings him into conflict with his own ideas of teaching and learning in this particular context. In the description of a lesson that follows, Andrew talks through his thinking and highlights the factors behind his decision making.

Table 7.1 outlines the structure and content of Andrew's lesson on the Andes conducted with a class of 13–14 year olds.

TABLE 7.1 Outline of Andrew's lesson on the Andes

Lesson episode	Brief description of activity
Starter activity, recap from previous lesson	Students recorded on mini-whiteboards the social, economic, and environmental advantages and disadvantages of tourism in a fold mountain region. Selected students fed their answers back to the group, through a teacher led recap.
Extended recap from previous lesson – focus on where and how the Andes are formed	Working in pairs, students had to discuss with each other where the Andes are and how they were formed (content covered in a previous lesson). Students were encouraged to mime the formation of fold mountains.
Atlas activity – describe the location of the Andes	Working in pairs with an atlas, students were required to write a 50-word description of the location of the Andes, with reference to key words such as longitude, latitude, tectonic plate, countries, continents, compass points. Examples were shared and discussed with the class.
Slide show with music and pictures of people living in the Andes	A slide show is presented with accompanying music from the Andes region. Whilst watching the images, students were asked to record how humans are using the land and what difficulties they may face. These observations are then shared with the class. Andrew asked questions to encourage the students to contrast what they had seen of the Andes with their previous case study of the Alps.

(continued)

TABLE 7.1 *(continued)*

Lesson episode	Brief description of activity
Ask the Expert using textbook spread	Using a double page textbook spread, five students were identified as Experts and asked to learn the information, whilst the rest of the group explore the information from the textbook to compose questions to ask the Experts. Experts are brought back into the room, sat at the front, to answer questions from the rest of the class. A score was kept as to whether the Experts were able to answer the questions.
Interrogation of a newspaper article on farming practices of the Incas	Students were given a newspaper article from *Argentina Independent*. The instructions were for them to: • Highlight words they did not understand • Describe the physical landscape • Find ways in which farming has been successful • Describe how farming takes place today. An extension question was provided: how has the land use changed?
Plenary – what skills have you learnt from learning toolkit?	Students respond to the plenary questions, using vocabulary from the school learning toolkit.

The students were active throughout the lesson, moving swiftly from one activity to the next and the level of engagement was high. The lesson used a range of different sources of geographical information: students' previous learning, an atlas, a textbook, and a newspaper article. Most of the interaction in the lesson was between students. As the teacher, Andrew did very little talking from the front, choosing to walk around the classroom, asking questions rather than engaging in direct instruction. In our discussion after the lesson, Andrew explained that his lesson planning had been dominated by two factors: an awareness that the students were likely to be restless and needed to be engaged with their work, and a need to ensure they had covered the content required by the examination specification. However, through our discussion, it also became clear that Andrew had other factors that affected his planning.

When describing the extended recap activity, Andrew's plan for the students to talk to each other was a deliberate behaviour management strategy:

> Mainly because I knew with that class, on a Wednesday afternoon, that some of them wouldn't listen. So they would actually gain more from telling their partner. Also I knew that they knew it, and understood it before, because I had been through their books. If I wasn't sure that they had understood it, then I wouldn't have done it in that way.

However, this approach, coupled with the pressure from the school to teach in a particular way, meant that Andrew had included activities in the lesson that he doubted had an educational value:

> So the textbook gives in-depth detail about the human land-uses of the Andes. The double page looks at forestry and farming. I find it difficult to think about interesting ways to communicate this sort of information to them. Part of me thinks that 'Ask the Expert' is a load of rubbish because it is just a memory test and so really are they learning anything? But I find that with classes like that, because they are very bright, and because it was only for a short amount of time, they read it and it is a sort of a game. Because it is competitive they do come up with quite interesting questions.

Andrew could justify the inclusion of this activity (which also illustrates his compliance with the school's preferred pedagogical approach) because it was balanced with other knowledge-based activities:

> I personally think that atlases are not really used enough in geography today. In other schools that I've been in, I don't think they really have that much of an understanding of where places are in the world and . . . I just think it's really important the students are able to actually locate the places that they are talking about before they learn about it. I want to link that to latitude and longitude (which they learn about in Year Seven) to keep up their skills. You know they struggled with that today and they used to be able to do that perfectly two years ago . . . I wanted them to keep using the kind of thinking, about describing places on a map, you know, using North, South, East and West. And thinking about which countries the Andes actually stretches across and actually being able to visualise how far they look across South America. So I think it's quite important for them to have the atlases and to work it out for themselves.

Andrew also designed the activities with an appreciation of what the students would need in order to be successful in the examination:

> I was trying to get them to think about using these high-level words. It seems that the difference between the A and A★ at GCSE is about using geographical terminology, linking ideas and linking economic-social-environment and those sort of things. So we try to get that in early on. Trying to get them to categorise ideas.

Andrew was also aware of the different ways that knowledge was being presented in the lesson:

> I wanted then to appreciate the Andes is different culturally to the Alps which they have been to and which we looked at. So the slide presentation

provided some images and music which suggest that perhaps the culture in this area is going to be different from the Alps. Previously we've looked at skiing in Switzerland and that kind of thing. They associate skiing with other white British people skiing, their dads having chalets and that kind of thing. So I want them to just have a kind of different stance.

He contrasts this with the use of more traditional resources like the newspaper article: 'I like them to use these articles, because they are complicated and it really does get them thinking – it is from the *Argentina Independent*, so it is a genuine article.' In addition, Andrew defends the use of traditional resources in preference to other technology:

> There has been a shift away from that kind of core knowledge and especially with things like Google Earth you don't necessarily know how to interpret maps in the same way or you don't need to maybe . . . I think the minute you get them on Google Earth they will fly from one place to another and they don't have that same sense of where it is in relation to the rest of the world. There are loads of advantages to Google Earth, I really like it. But it doesn't necessarily give you that real sense of space I guess, but not in terms of one place in relation to the other.

There is a layering of information in this lesson. The paired work at the start connects the students with previous learning; the focus on locational knowledge is then supplemented with the introduction of new information through three authoritative sources: the slide show, the textbook, and the newspaper article. Andrew's role as the teacher here is to act as a curator of knowledge: he selects and presents information, and offers students an activity to engage them with that information. This process can be seen as a form of recontextualizing knowledge, as he brings in information from a variety of sources to piece together the learning in the lesson. The learning approach was for students to extract relevant information from the various sources in a variety of ways. Andrew orchestrated feedback from the students, asked them challenging questions to extend their answers, and offered them guidance and provided task instruction. However, at no point in the lesson did Andrew stand at the front and talk to the class about the Andes. There was no teacher exposition or direct instruction in the lesson. In the light of his articulation of his preferred approaches and ideas about learning geography, this seemed odd. Andrew explained how he felt his old geography teachers would have responded to this lesson:

> I think that some of the activities I used they would have been on board with, things like the newspaper article; they would have liked that. The kind of thing that was very engaging – so the paired work, talking, that kind of thing – they would have used those sorts of things. I suppose their teaching changed a lot over the last couple of years because they began to get on board with some of the ideas. I think that there was core knowledge in the

lesson. I don't think it was all process because there were concrete facts about the Andes and about the formation of fold mountains. They have gained a kind of sense of the culture. They can incorporate facts and figures out of the expert activity and the newspaper article so I think that the actual content was there in terms of how people are using the Andes but I suppose it was more all singing and all dancing compared with perhaps some of the methods that would have been used.

I asked Andrew if he had deliberately chosen not to talk from the front in the lesson:

Yes I planned not to do that. Because it's what I have been told to do. In all the observations I've had here, I've been pulled up for talking too much and they are trying to hone in on this massive shift: 'they should be doing more work than you', 'you shouldn't be lecturing from the front', 'they should be doing activity, activity, activity'.

As a result of this focus, Andrew admitted to looking around for alternative sources of knowledge, feeling unable to speak to his students himself.

In some ways because I feel like I wouldn't be able to stand at the front and just tell them about the Andes, because you can't do that, because you're not allowed . . . so I think you have to think of different ways. So in a lesson plan, if I was to justify my lesson, we have been told that the emphasis is on the learning rather than the teaching. So if you are observing a lesson, you have to write down what learning is taking place and I suppose learning can't possibly be just listening and writing things down.

Nuanced decision making

There were aspects of Andrew's lesson that reflected the school's preferred approach to lessons: no direct instruction, a variety of active-learning and group-based activities and focussing on the student as knower as well as learner. Andrew's own practice can also be seen as adhering to the advice he received from lesson observations: he did not talk from the front and did use 'Ask an Expert' activities. This is not to say, however, that Andrew has adopted all the school's directives uncritically. For example, whilst he had the lesson objectives written on an early PowerPoint slide, he did not adopt the school approach to their use, which was to have them on every slide. He did include another recently introduced whole-school policy – the learners' toolkit – in his lesson, despite being sceptical about its value and what the students gain from it: 'They don't know what that means, and how it has applied to the lesson; they have just learnt the terms from the back of their book and repeat it as an answer.'

This kind of decision making is high-stakes for Andrew, and he is aware of what the consequences of not teaching in the way the school expects him to can be. He outlines how he has heard of disciplinary action being taken against colleagues for not falling in line. He also highlights the significance of his observation grades in relation to the opportunity to receive salary enhancements through performance-related pay. Such a context does not leave him with much room to enact his professional judgement. He discussed his frustration with not being able to voice his critique of the approaches being promoted:

> I think the difference is that where some of these external people they come in with a really one-minded viewpoint and they've got a really fixed idea of how things should be done. So they come into school and think 'wow, this isn't being done the right way – let's change it. You have to do it like this' . . . It does frustrate me because I think that perhaps some people have got the context of the school a bit wrong and may be there isn't really a one-size-fits-all model for teaching and learning. I think you have to really look at the environment and adapt things.

In response, Andrew has adopted a nuanced approach to resisting and complying with the school culture. In some areas he falls in with the teaching and learn-ing approaches of the school culture; in others, areas that he perceives as being more 'high stakes' (to the learning of geography), he challenges these dominant approaches. The decisions that he makes are grounded in his practice and appear to be based on a moral reasoning. Where the stakes are high, such as with A level teaching, he is prepared to take more of a risk, to assert what he believes is more appropriate teaching and learning. He is more likely to comply when he is able to work around the policy (through using different teaching and learning strategies), or when the lesson is seen as having lower stakes.

Part of Andrew's professional identity is formed from a heighted form of 'constituent knowledge' (Heilbronn and Yandell 2010), knowledge about the specific context of the school that emerges from his long relationship with it, and in particular the extent to which he identifies with being a pupil:

> I can relate so well to the boys because I can specifically remember what it was like to be them. I can picture myself. I was taught in the room that I teach in. So I really know which bits they are going to hate and which bits they will enjoy and that gives me quite a unique perspective.

Andrew is able to present a coherent argument for why certain approaches are not appropriate in this school context:

> A lot of these methods really do work for inner-city schools and for schools where kids find it difficult to learn. Where they have got completely differ-ent abilities, you do have to implement some of these methods because if you stand at the front you probably wouldn't get through to some of them because they wouldn't be engaged. But I think that in some ways you have

to take the context into consideration. I mean, what's the point of teaching
A level geography to kids that are going to Cambridge in September like that?
When for the next three years they are listening and they will get lectured at.
Because you haven't really prepared them for that at all.

Andrew's vision of how the students feel and act clearly influences his ideas about
teaching and learning. However, these are being challenged by the changing school
culture. The dilemma that Andrew articulates is between this idealized vision of
the school (which may or may not be a true representation of it but is derived
from his own experience of having been a student there) and the pressures that he
experiences to teach in a particular way.

Subject identity and the classroom

Andrew's case shows how the sacred stories from the professional knowledge landscape can filter down into the classroom. The debates about what is the best way
to teach his students and the significance of the context and recent history of the
school are key to understanding Andrew's practice. The classroom can be seen as
the site where these dilemmas are played out. Andrew's narrative shows how his
decision making about these issues is grounded in the high stakes nature of his lessons, for himself as a teacher and for his students.

His subject story, particularly his recognition of himself as a grammar school
geographer, offers a lens through which he positions himself in the debates taking
place within the school. This subject story appears to be a key feature of his subject
identity and the values that underpin his teaching practice.

What also emerges here is the degree to which Andrew feels he is able to
express his professional judgement – more in some contexts than he is able to in
others. He has a sense of what direction he wishes his practice to go in, but feels
that he is being pulled in different directions by the events happening in the school,
which in turn have been influenced by the changes in the broad education culture.
In some cases he is willing and able to express his resistance to these approaches,
but he is not whole-heartedly against them, nor does he see them as negative.
His perspective is balanced, but the school approach is not, and this affects how
Andrew feels about working within this school culture. His professional practice
can be seen as deliberate and guided by his subject identity.

Andrew's case is unusual due to his extended knowledge of the school in question and, no doubt, this affects how Andrew feels about changes being introduced
under the new school leadership. He is also keenly aware of the importance of being
seen to comply with school policies whilst at the same time having a strong sense of
what is needed for his students to have a good quality geography education.

Other teachers may not experience the same degree of contrasting advice that
Andrew has articulated. But this is what makes Andrew's case an interesting one.
By using the professional knowledge landscape and professional compass meta-
phor, we can build a picture of Andrew's practice as navigating a way through a

series of conflicting expectations about teaching, some of which he does not agree with. The idea of navigation is important. To navigate this landscape, Andrew needs to have a detailed understanding of what the landscape looks like: he needs to understand the 'lay of the land' and also the destination he is navigating towards. Some of this information is provided by the school, through its sacred stories. But some is also part of what Andrew brings to the landscape in the shape of his own conceptions and ideas of what it means to teach and learn geography well.

However, having a detailed understanding of the landscape is only part of the picture. Andrew also needs a clear sense of where he is situated within it. In other words, Andrew has a clear idea of how he feels about certain policies and preferred practices. He also has an image of himself as a geography teacher and the practices associated with that. In this lesson we have seen how he moves between these different images: how he navigates between them. How he chooses to react is guided, at least in part, by his professional compass.

Note

1 Both the National Literacy Strategy and the Numeracy Strategy were introduced by the government in 1998 to improve the teaching of literacy and numeracy in schools.

8

SUBJECT IDENTITY THROUGH A CAREER

So far I have outlined how the professional compass is a useful way to understand teachers' practice and how and why they behave in the way they do. But how can this idea be of help in addressing the problem of teacher attrition. There are a number of reasons why teachers leave the profession, but we know very little about how and why some teachers stay. The aging workforce is a key concern for many countries, as established and experienced teachers are approaching retirement. If the professional compass is important to teachers' day to day practice and resilience, it may also be a sustaining influence throughout their career.

Dan, the teacher who features in this chapter, was one of the first teachers I interviewed (in 2003). I interviewed Dan again in 2014. Dan was one of the teachers with the strongest sense of identity who took part in this research. He had a clear sense of his strengths as a teacher and his reasons for maintaining an interest in geography. Interviewing him 11 years later revealed the consistency of these values. Dan was also one of the happiest and most fulfilled teachers I talked to, and whilst it would be presumptive to connect his strong sense of identity and his contentment with his career, it does raise the question of how having a strong professional compass might be a sustaining influence for teachers, and make them more likely to stay in the profession.

Throughout this book we have reflected on Clandinin and Connelly's (1995) emphasis on the dynamic nature of professional knowledge landscapes. The contexts and official discourses that affect teaching can be differently interpreted in different places but, of course, can also change over time. How teachers respond to that changing professional knowledge landscape can vary depending on their own values and sense of purpose. This is of course, the same over time too. In Chapter Six we saw how both Mandy and Daisy had adapted to different contexts, and the variable impact this had on them individually. But how does this work as teachers near the end of their career? Steven, whose narrative we met at the start of this book, had chosen to leave teaching geography and to work in other aspects of education. Dan has chosen to stay.

This chapter brings together all three scales of the education, school and classroom contexts and introduces a new narrative to explore how they work together. The argument developed in this chapter is that a teacher's subject story can play a key part in professional identity, bringing coherence to professional practice. The subject story represents what it means for that individual to think through their subject. For the teacher, it can be seen as a threshold concept (Meyer and Land 2005) which is transformative, irreversible and integrative. This chapter shows how subject identity can be a tool in meaning making, showing direction and offering support when professional practice is challenged, and one that can last through a career, acting then like a professional compass. The person who is the focus of this chapter, Dan, tells a remarkable story of how a clear subject story can influence an entire career of professional practice.

Dan's subject story

At the time of the first interview Dan was Head of Geography at a school in a small town. He had been teaching for 14 years, and held a Masters degree in geography.

Dan's subject story stems from his desire 'to see things differently', a term he repeated throughout his interviews. This is reflected in his own experience as a learner and as a teacher. The desire to see things differently began with his school experiences of geography, when he studied the Schools Council 16–19 geography course and enjoyed the issues-based approach of the course.

Dan elaborates on how it was both the content and the style of the 16–19 course that inspired him:

> The issues-based thing was crucial really and it really got me going actually. All the time we would be looking at: 'should the bypass be built here' and that kind of thing. And we did a DME[1] and we went on fieldwork as well, which for everyone was a factor you know. And so we looked at: 'should they build a Pontins at the top of the cliff at Weymouth?' and things like that, and arguments for and against, and I really, really liked that. In fact, for quite a long time through my degree course, it was issues based in planning that actually I thought was my main interest. And it led me to choose planning options.

Dan was inspired by the approach of the 16–19 course which focused on geographical enquiry and issues. He reflects on the reasons for enjoying the course:

> I liked the intellectual challenge of that kind of thing. It was that element of challenge, of problem solving, that we are supposed to include to encourage in boys, aren't we? And it encouraged me. I did like the fact that the issues were political issues, like 'should we cut the rainforest down?' The London Docklands was one thing that really got me going actually with the political thing. It was in 1984, and it was just starting up, and we went to London

Docklands for a day. And I was really enthused by this Thatcherite sort of monstrosity that was developing. And all these people who were missing out on the redevelopment that was going on and that kind of thing. Seeing graffiti with 'LDDC out' and that kind of thing . . . I have always been interested in the issues and the slightly political side of things, and something to get your teeth into.

Dan links the political approach in geography to his interests at the time. He has already used the term 'seeing things differently' and this, he reflects, is a key part of his personality:

I had a very conservative upbringing with my family in suburban London, and I was looking generally as a person to stretch out and to get interested in different things than I had grown up with. I wore different clothes, and I watched different films, and it was a whole different way of learning and a whole different approach to the world, you know, deconstructing the iconography of things.

At university, the influence of the cultural geographer, Denis Cosgrove, enabled Dan to maintain his interest in geography by encouraging him to look at things in a different way:

It drew together some other interests of mine. I had done RE and English A level and I remember a very key moment, when I did a lecture and a seminar following it, done by Denis Cosgrove which was about post-modernism. And we were talking about language and its meaning and stuff like that and I just loved it. You know, of all the academic experience, learning experiences, that I have had that would stand out as being, you know, the thing that really got me going. Because it was challenging and it was different, I think.

I encouraged Dan to consider what other influences had affected his changing interest in geography. Unlike the other teachers, travel does not appear to have been a great influence on Dan, but, one fieldtrip experience had offered him an opportunity to see things in a different way:

I went to Gambia on a fieldtrip and that had quite an impact on me. Just seeing somewhere that is so different and made me reflect more on England and what that is like and again, more interested in places and so they were influences but not as major as the academic side of it really.

These influences have continued to affect how he perceives geography:

As a geographer? Well my main interest is in fieldwork and for the academic side of things I am very interested in the qualitative ways of doing fieldwork and I suppose it is drawing on the cultural geography interest and background but taking it into the fieldwork area, finding different ways of doing things and looking at the world in a different way. Again with a slightly post-modern approach if you like, and that would be my main drive and interest really.

Here we can see the transformative nature of his subject story, which appears to be acting as a lens through which he views his professional practice. Thinking in a different way appears to be synonymous with what it means to think geographically, for Dan. However, it is not the only influence on his practice.

In terms of how this subject story is reflected in his desire to teach geography, Dan outlined how he continued to feel a tension between time constraints and his desire to intellectually challenge his students. This had led him to develop strategies to enable him to work efficiently but also to get good results:

> I think I have got academic ability and the way that my brain works does help at times, so I think I have got quite a clear way of thinking and so when it comes down to breaking up difficult ideas at A level, for example, and making them straightforward and simple and logical.

He achieves this by considering what his students need and then planning accordingly. His ability to do this has been identified by Ofsted inspectors:

> Certainly an Ofsted inspector said to me recently I know what is important and I work on that and I hadn't really thought of that before but I think it is probably true and I try to . . . I recognise, for example, that if you are going to do well at GCSE they have to be able to write ten lines really well, getting in examples and developing their points and I just really, really flog that and I have loads of ways of doing that.

Dan has an efficient and focused approach to planning. He offers an analogy to explain this further:

> Yeah, it's like the grand prix driver that is supposed to win the race in the slowest possible time, because if you go racing ahead your car might break up and I think, and I have learnt very, very slowly, because it is not in my nature really, that I tend to be a bit of a perfectionist, or used to be. I am not anymore because wiser older teachers have taught me to get out of school as soon as possible and to get home and to see the kids and to try not to work in the evenings if you can. When things are important, do them well but when they are not, can they be left?

Such a view makes it more important for Dan to have a clear perspective on what he wants to achieve. The desire to see things in a different way is evident when he discusses why geography is important for students:

> I think it is important to know about the world they live in. Very often I find that I am teaching something and I think, I am glad they are learning

this, I am glad that they are becoming aware of this and I think it is important. Like, for example, trade, and why some countries are rich and some are poor.

He is also critical of a purely utilitarian approach to education:

> I think that it is a shame if you are just doing things preparing them for work all the time – I think that we would end up a very shallow society . . . but my education was not very much preparing me for work directly but the things I gained most from education were things like an understanding of the world around me, things that I know about, the apartheid system and what happened there, for example, and I feel that I am a better person for that. Also, this approach that cultural geography gives on looking at the world in a different way and with a different slant on things and it has influenced me all the time and the way that I look at things . . . geography can do that kind of thing.

This tension between the influences from the education context and the desire to intellectually challenge his students is something that Dan is keenly aware of:

> I try but I mean, more in KS3 than KS4 and A level because I keep finding myself becoming a bit of an exam factory to be honest. I've become quite good at getting kids through exams and hopefully some of that seeing the world in a different way is a by-product . . . If there is an exam that we have got to get them through. I'll get them through as well as I can because I feel a responsibility to them and so that has got to be my priority.

In his practice, he also describes using geography as a way of mediating broader educational influences, to ensure that the students benefit:

> In fact, I'm not really bothered about what the content is too much anyway, I've made sure we cover the National Curriculum roughly but with our Year 9 exam work, for example, I can't even remember what we are supposed to do on Japan but we make sure that they know a few important features about Japan and also their literacy develops when they do Japan – that is the thing that we really work on.

His subject story enables him to make curriculum decisions. Dan had also developed a particular expertise in geographical fieldwork, inspired by a colleague who had an interest in sustainable development. This green perspective shares similar features to his desire to see things in a different way:

> . . . they bring me further towards a different take on life, probably a little more politicised and a bit less materialistic . . . I think when your outlook on life comes through your teaching which it does quite a lot and it has.

For example, I was teaching about Slapton yesterday about the road on the shingle ridge and how it has eroded and probably my slant on it was more towards the environmental approach.

Dan's interest in fieldwork was the subject of a Best Practice Research Scholarship (funding by the DfES for practising teachers to develop a piece of action research in an area of best practice for wide dissemination). In this work he pulled together his interests in literacy and qualitative fieldwork:

Qualitative fieldwork, on the other hand, I have found has got its limitations as well, so, you can have a great time setting up haiku poems and stuff like that but I am wondering where you can take them, what you can do with them, I want to give them a bit more structure.

The focus on fieldwork has brought together many of the geographical and educational interests that stimulate him:

Also I was thinking if I could bring in some of this Socratic dialogue thing that Denis Cosgrove wrote about, and used with his students in Venice trying to challenge the way that the children think about the place in a completely different way. You know what would happen if there were no cars here? For example, how would it be different? And challenge the assumptions that they would have. So I have ended up with a whole model/approach to fieldwork and I want to try and publish it.

Dan's subject identity is dominated by this subject story of seeing things in a different way. This subject story is a driver in his professional practice outside the classroom, but was also reflected in the lessons I observed him teach.

Dan's professional practice

To appreciate the consistency of Dan's subject identity, it is useful to see how it worked within his classroom practice. The following lesson was observed in 2003 when I first watched Dan teach. It was with a Year 11 geography GCSE group. The aim of this lesson was to compare the eruption of Nevado del Ruiz to that of Mount St Helens. This aim was expressed as a question that formed the title of the lesson: 'Why was the Nevado del Ruiz in Colombia more destructive than Mount St Helens?' The lesson featured a range of ways to prepare for the pending examination, but was underpinned by a view of thinking geographically which was concerned with getting the students to think in a different way.

The lesson began with the students arriving from break, and Dan greeted them at the door using lots of praise and thanks and giving jobs to the early arrivals. At the start of the lesson he thanked those who had handed out resources, then introduced the lesson by informing the class that they were going to look at a different volcano. He introduced the main question and made it clear that the lesson emphasis was on why this eruption was worse. He set up the purpose of the lesson by explaining that although the size of the eruption was not very different, the effects were and they were going to find out why. He outlined that they would be watching a video, answering questions and then they would end with an exam question. I noted in my research diary, that he made the objective of the lesson '*really* clear'.

He began the lesson by asking the students to highlight the main points that they had covered in a previous lesson on Mount St Helens. As they did this, he focused them on the key themes that were relevant to this lesson. He directed his comments to individuals, e.g. 'Heidi: focus on these ideas'. He then outlined key factors about the location of Nevado del Ruiz and introduced a three-minute news clip of the eruption, asking the students to focus on why it was so devastating (again, emphasizing the lesson objective). Whilst they watched the video clip, he wrote the main title and paragraph headings on the board:

The eruption
Reasons for the large number of fatalities
Rescue attempts
Longer term.

Once the video clip was finished, he drew these 'themes' to the class's attention. The themes represented the key elements of information featured in the lesson and became themes for the learning to take place. The class then examined one of the newspaper clippings that had been handed out. As the students interrogated these clippings, he asked them to respond to the main themes he had identified. The following dialogue demonstrates how he developed the students' ideas:

Student 1:	The expertise was there but it was ignored.
Dan:	Why would they want to do that?
Student 1:	Would it cost money?
Dan:	What is the main economy there?
Student 1:	Tourism?
Dan:	Is it too remote?
Student 1:	Farming, all the field crops will have gone, there will be no money.
Dan:	Good, where is this place?
Student 1:	In a valley.
Dan:	Why do they live there?
Student 1:	That's where the water is.
Dan:	Brilliant, you are really thinking.

Dan's questioning approach was designed to get his students thinking and engaging with the resources. They then looked at another textbook resource and summarized the content. The reading was focused and directed, highlighting the relevant factors within each paragraph. He made reference to their impending examination by reminding them: 'Facts and figures; keep the examiner happy.' He also encouraged good behaviour: 'Be polite: that would be really nice.'

The remainder of the lesson was dedicated to the other resources that they had been given. He highlighted which resources were harder to read and asked them to interrogate the resources to find additional information under the appropriate headings, again referring them to the main question. During this main part of the lesson, he walked around the class, offering support and encouragement; this was again directed at the main question, and examination techniques: 'Brilliant, excellent, now give me the details. That's what the examiner wants.'

In the last part of the lesson, he thanked the students for their attention and praised them on the process that they had just gone through. He then encouraged them to share the main points they had made. During this feedback he continually brought them back to the main question and asked them to compare what they had found out from this case study with what they knew about the Mount St Helens' eruption. He also asked for specific detail, reminding them of what would be expected by the examiners.

In this lesson, Dan emphasizes how his students could prepare for the examination whilst also tries to extend and challenge them. He makes nuanced decisions, maintaining his own professional priorities but balancing them against pressures from the school. The pedagogy he has chosen reflects this pragmatic approach, but is also underpinned by his subject epistemology – an understanding that thinking geographically and seeing things in a different way are synonymous.

The continuity of subject identity and professional practice

In 2014, I interviewed Dan again. He had moved from the school where he had taught to a Sixth Form College in a neighbouring town. His move to the Sixth Form College (he had been teaching there for eight years at the time of our conversation) was because he had 'got bored of teaching KS3', in particular the lack of variety in the curriculum and having to teach all the year groups meant that he felt he could not spend sufficient time 'jazzing it up'. In particular, however, he emphasized how he had started to appreciate that he liked teaching examination classes. He found that the focus on exams had meant he could focus on his teaching. In his previous school he had 'enjoyed teaching A level – and I love it now'.

Dan elaborated on how the teaching of A level had changed over the years:

> I've changed to teaching A level only – there are different demands. Results are so important – that's still a focus. Obviously, it is also important to prepare people for university and to make sure they develop the skills and all that . . . The bottom line is that they have to get these results. It is important for everyone. It is devastating if someone needs an A grade to get into Sheffield, and they desperately want to go to Sheffield and then they get a B and so they can't go.

The previous driver that we discussed – wanting his students to see things in a different way – was still important to him: 'The aim is to get the results in place and then we can do what we want to do – we can go deeper into some things; to some extent they marry together.' He offered examples of his practice, such as a recent day trip to look at social segregation in a major nearby city and how the focus of the fieldwork had been on helping students to see the city in a different way (with an emphasis on the different ethnic communities) but also to support them in their examination preparations.

Dan discussed how one of the things from the education policies that had particularly influenced his practice had been the focus on assessment for learning (AfL). He outlined the strategies that had now become a regular part of his practice:

> I use AfL hugely, particularly the modelling of paragraphs and that sort of thing. For example, I use coloured highlighter pens for marking: green is for good, pink is for think and so they have to think about what the pink is for – why did I highlight it? So I use AfL a lot, it is good for them – an important theory.

However, he was dismissive of other drivers in education. His school had recently experienced an Ofsted inspection, but the effect had been minimal on him: 'We didn't tip into silliness. We gradually prepared, and so there was not much pressure. We had been advised to do certain things but there was not much extra work, and we were ready. Some [other departments] went nuts.' He attributes this to a confidence in his practice and those of his department colleagues: 'we know what we are doing is good so we didn't panic.'

In terms of the school culture, Dan was keen to highlight how different he found working in a post-16 college to a school. He outlined that he had more autonomy in his practice, and because of this the teachers 'demand to be treated more like grown-ups'. He explained how this had affected attempts to change the working practices of the institution: 'There is a strong union here and the staff will fight. The management tried to do things but they struggled – so they suggested learning walks and the staff went ballistic.'

However, some of the mediating influences that Dan had outlined before continued to drive his practice. He described the department as 'driven' but also 'We do cut corners – all over the place – but nothing that is important'. The terminology he used in this part of his narrative directly echoed, word-for-word, what he had said to me 11 years before. The ability to make decisions and to determine what is important has enabled Dan to focus on aspects of his practice that he wants to prioritize: specifically, focussing on examination success and challenging his students to think differently. His practice is still underpinned by the same subject story: he has focused on how to enable his students to achieve examination success, but this is underpinned by what it means to think geographically and to see things in a different way.

One area where there had been significant change for Dan is with his work on qualitative fieldwork. Whilst he still discussed this work as a guest lecturer at a local university (which he described as his 'favourite day of the year') he felt that the relevance of the work had passed: 'Fieldwork stuff: I think I reached the extent of it – there's nothing more to do.' He described how young geographers and geography teachers he met were already informed about qualitative fieldwork techniques and so the need to promote and develop this area had now passed (although he did feel there was still some place for recognition of the approach by the examination board).

> Qualitative fieldwork – I took it as far as I could go and thoroughly explored all the possibilities. I'm happy now with what is going on. I squeezed as much as I could out of it. I do reflect on it every year when I do that day in [local university]. But there is not much more to do . . . there is only so far as you can take it. I talk to young teachers now and they have come across it and done it themselves and teachers are open to it. So I don't feel the need any more because things have changed – and the demand to do it isn't there.

Dan did outline a new area of geographical interest, to do with segregation in the city, but described this as a focus on the changing A level curriculum. However, this interest was very much tied in with his current role.

One of the key themes here is the enduring nature of Dan's subject identity. In many ways one could view Dan's professional practice as having created his own niche, building on his strengths (and motivations) as a teacher, Dan has developed a role for himself where he has freed himself from the influences he does not like and has been able to focus on those areas he does enjoy. Of course, it is not possible to determine that Dan's current position, his career path and current emotional state are all due to the strength of his subject identity, but what we can see is that he has made decisions at both a career level and a class-room level that have been in line with his ideas and beliefs about teaching and his view of the subject. Working with this subject identity has proved to be fulfilling and rewarding for him. In his own words: 'Coming here was the death of ambition – because I am so happy and fulfilled.'

Subject identity as a sustaining influence

I have focused on the decisions that Dan has made through his career and in his practice as a way of showing how his professional identity appears to be related to his subject identity. The values that he has developed about geography, why geography is important to teach and to learn, and the contribution that the subject can make to a young person's education, incorporate many aspects of his professional practice – how he structures his lessons, how he makes decisions about his career, what he emphasizes in his own classroom and in his leadership of others. All of these are driven by Dan's professional principles: making a difference and enabling students to be successful. I suggest that these are driven by his understanding of what it means to think (and learn) geographically. This analysis illustrates that these principles appear to be related to his subject identity and subject story. Dan's awakening as a thinking person, and in particular in thinking about things in a different way, stemmed from his initial engagement with the subject, though his motivation continued throughout his career. These professional values can also be seen as subject values, as they originated from Dan's early engagement with the subject and have played an important role in guiding him.

Throughout this part, I have described this influence of subject identity as acting like a professional compass. The fact that this term has a moral implication is deliberate. Teachers have different degrees of autonomy afforded to them by their school contexts. These school contexts act as landscapes of professional practice and, of course, can vary widely: curricula change, examination specifications change, and teachers' autonomy to choose what to teach and how can change. Teachers can use their subject identity to help them navigate those landscapes.

In the previous chapters, the different narratives have shown how this can work in a number of ways, including at a range of different scales of professional practice and at different points through a teacher's own career. In addition, the narratives are affected by the contexts that teachers work in and how these contexts interplay with their identities, and how this can affect classroom practice. The focus of this chapter has been at more of a temporal scale: how this can change over time. Dan's story would suggest that making decisions which are in line with values of a subject story can sustain teachers throughout their careers. In the light of the teacher recruitment crisis, this would seem to be a significant finding. But it may also be an unusual one.

Generalizations about a person's career and the root of their motivation need to be treated with some caution. Not all teachers who remain in the profession can attest to such a happy and contented working life. It also does not necessarily follow that teachers should have complete professional autonomy. What stands out for me about Dan's story is how he has changed schools at a time when he was looking for a different type of professional experience. In other words, knowing when to move into different roles and positions and selecting those in a way that chimes with professional identity and practice can be seen as an important part of how subject identity can sustain professional practice through a career.

There are echoes here of the importance of timing that featured in the previous narratives. Mandy's context also appears to be right for her at that particular stage of her career. Paul and Nicola were also happy with their school contexts and the challenges they offered. Daisy, on the other hand, was working in a context that did not suit her, but that she acknowledged might suit other, less experienced, teachers. This adds a further dimension to our understanding of the relationship between context and identity and the importance of moving on at the right time. The issue of context then is also about timing.

Note

1 DME: Decision Making Exercise.

9

A PROFESSIONAL COMPASS

If teachers can be seen as working in professional knowledge landscapes, then they need a professional compass to navigate those landscapes. In this book, the argument has been made that teachers' values, particularly those that have come from their subject identities, are a key part of that professional compass. When faced with challenges, from their school context and broader educational reforms, teachers can use this professional compass to guide them in how they respond. But the professional compass is just a metaphor to explain why teachers behave in the way they do. In this chapter, I outline why this is a useful idea for understanding teachers' personal and emotional lives, and for understanding teacher professionalism and the politics that surround teachers' work, but also for thinking about teacher development. I return to some of the themes and ideas explored throughout this book, in particular the interplay between contexts and identities and the idea of pedagogical content knowledge and recontextualization, and illustrate why taking a values perspective can lead to a deeper understanding of teachers' work.

The argument developed throughout this book has been that teacher subject identity can be an important part of professional identity and a powerful influence on professional practice. The data taken from a range of geography teachers illustrate the unique and individual ways that teachers can recount and use their subject identities, and the differing degrees to which they can influence their practice. The importance of subject identity is that it emphasizes the moral and ethical dimensions of a teacher's work. Subject identity is part of professional identity, and can also be linked to personal identity. The metaphor of a professional compass can help to illustrate how this can influence professional practice.

The metaphor of a professional compass is similar to the popular metaphor of a moral compass. The function of a compass is to point the user towards north. The compass user can then use this sense of direction to orientate themselves: to determine their current location, identify their destination and decide how to navigate the route between those two points. The compass does not prescribe which route is to be taken nor where the final destination is likely to be. To be used effectively, the compass also requires an accurate map, preferably with some defining landmarks. To relate this metaphor to a teaching context, a professional compass will not necessarily determine which decisions the teacher should make, the desired learning outcomes or the curriculum goals they are working towards. The teacher will need to understand their own particular professional landscapes, but can determine the direction of travel.

Teachers' professional and personal identities

To understand how the professional compass works, it has to be seen within the context of identity and identity formation. Since the 1980s there has been a growth of interest in identity studies in a range of disciplinary fields. Combining the findings from psychological, philosophical, anthropological (Beauchamp and Thomas 2009) and socio- and cultural studies has yielded a complex but valuable understanding of how teachers make sense of their professional work and practice.

One of the key themes to emerge from the literature on teachers' identity is the importance of a teacher's concept of self. Firstly, there is a need to distinguish between a teacher's personal and professional identities. Particularly in their early development, teachers need to develop their concept of themselves as a teacher through connecting personal and professional aspects of their identities (Meijer *et al.* 2009). Pre-service teachers do not necessarily begin with an image of themselves as teachers, and Danielewicz (1995) argues that becoming a teacher means that an individual must adopt an identity which requires the development of personal theories of action. The personal nature of these theories of action illustrates that developing a teacher identity is highly individualized, as it requires teachers to explore aspects of their personal identity. These aspects of personal identity may include dimensions such as gender, social class (Van Galen 2010), politics (Huddy 2001) or religious affiliation (White 2009) and also beliefs about teaching and what it means to them to become a teacher. Teacher identity can also include how it feels to be a teacher in the classroom. Identity formation therefore requires imagination (Trent and Lim 2010) and a negotiation between both personal and professional identities (which Alsup (2005) highlights can also be distinct from each other). Alsup describes these identities as 'discursive borderlands'. Whilst there is a ready made set of teacher identities (or images) available to teachers (such as those from popular culture and our own experiences of education), Søreide (2006) argues that putting them into effect produces different ontological narratives.

One of these narratives is that of subject identity, a neglected aspect of the research on teacher identity. The neglect of subject identity is significant because, when someone decides they want to become a teacher of a subject (or a particular phase), they will already have fairly clear images of what teaching that subject (or phase) will look like. But how these idealized images of teaching can affect the identity formation of teachers is an emotional and highly individualized process

(Zemblyas 2003) and it involves resistance, transformation and compliance as individuals juggle with alternative images and conceptions of what it means to be a teacher. This is particularly the case when teachers find themselves behaving in ways that may not match up to their image of the teacher they want to be. The pressure to behave in a certain way that is contrary to your own values, may lead teachers to feel disempowered. In this way teachers can feel as if they are a sub-ordinated group, disempowered to act autonomously. Such feelings of being disempowered or deprofessionalized can lead people to behave in particular ways as Andrew Sayer (2005: 160) explains:

> The struggle of subordinated groups for self-respect is particularly likely to lead to contradictory dispositions and opinions. They may try to make a virtue out of their position and their toughness and fortitude in bearing burdens, at the same time as they feel shame about having to bear those burdens. These are simultaneously responses of resistance and compliance.

Teachers can justify particular actions in the light of what they perceive is needed, expected or required. The process is therefore one of continual negotiation.

Such continual negotiation or, to borrow from Barnett, 'being a teacher' can be seen in the narratives discussed in the previous chapters, where teachers negotiate their sense of the teacher they want to be, with the reforms and contexts that are influencing their work. For some this can feel like a highly personal struggle.

So to understand the professional compass and how it can influence teachers' work, it is important to see it as part of the transition between teachers' personal and professional identities. Bérci (2006) notes how important it is for teachers to integrate self into their work if they are to move beyond teaching as a technical or mechanical act. Aspects of teachers' personal lives will therefore affect their work. These observations are supported by much work into how teachers' values affect their practice (Council of Europe 1985; Dunne and Wragg 1994; Starratt 1994; Thompson 1995; Kyriacou 1997) and their classroom environments (Mortimore *et al.* 1988). Teachers' opinions and beliefs reflect their unique range of experiences and perspectives but it is not always possible to distinguish between the professional and personal values of teachers as both will affect their practice (Van Mannen 1995; Carr 2006). Whilst Friedman's (2006) work acknowledges that they can be conflicting, values always affect the cognitive domain and so will affect teachers' practice right down to deciding what to teach (Slater 1996).

This recognition of the centrality of teachers' values emphasizes their emotional investment in their work. Teaching is acknowledged as an emotional activity (Bullough and Draper 2004), and the classroom is the main site for teachers' self-esteem and fulfilment, which in turn can affect their understanding of their practice (van Veen and Lasky 2005) and their emotions about teaching (for example, through experiencing guilt (Hargreaves 1994)). Teachers are required to engage in emotional relationships with several groups of people (including colleagues, students and parents) (Hargreaves 2001). Teachers work at these relationships and they reflect the personal nature of teaching and how it can affect the way a teacher interacts with others. At the core of this investment then are the values that drive a teacher's professional practice (Korthagen 2004).

Korthagen suggests that teacher identity encompasses a series of levels, nested like the layers of an onion (2004). The central components of mission and identity influence the beliefs of a teacher, which in turn will translate into their practice and behaviour. Related to this deep sense of mission is the idea that teaching is a moral activity (Campbell et al. 2004). This has been identified in much work on teaching (see Campbell 2003) and reflected in the recognition of the bi-polar nature of teaching, between mission and power (Friedman 2006).

One of the debates in this area that has yet to be resolved is the transient or permanent nature of the influence of teachers' identities on their practice. Fang (1996) refers to this as the two competing theses – consistency and inconsistency: that teachers' identities appear to be both stable and dynamic at the same time. It is not therefore enough to look at who a person is; the contexts they have found themselves in and how this has affected their values and beliefs, and also where these values and beliefs come from and why they are meaningful to the teacher must also be examined. The subject stories retold in earlier chapters reveal the complexity of this interplay between context and identity and how the alignment of values is central to the impact they can have on individuals.

Teacher development

Throughout this book, I have emphasized that values are an implicit part of teacher professional practice. However, they are also a significantly neglected part of teacher development. Although the exhibition of professional values is often seen as a key part of teacher certification and qualification, the definition of those values is often more in line with professional conduct or with an ethical code, rather than with the particular values of individual teachers. This is not to say that the importance of teacher values has not been recognized. Indeed, it has been widely recognized that an understanding of teachers' values is an important part of appreciating how they understand and relate to their subject knowledge (Grossman et al. 1989; Gudmundsdottir 1990; 1991b). The dimension that has been emphasized here is that these values often have a subject dimension: they are grounded in what it is about the subject that appeals to individual teachers. In the case of geography, Alun Morgan (2011) has described this as geo-ethics, but one could also argue that there are science-ethics, history-ethics and so on. Having a detailed understanding, through the lens of a discipline, changes how one views and values the world and undoubtedly in the case of teachers will affect how they teach about it.

But attention to subject or disciplinary values is not always a strong feature of initial teacher education. The teachers in this research connected with the subject at different points of time. For Paul it was before he had encountered the subject of geography at school; for others like Dan and Daisy it was much later in their school careers, when an aspect of school geography connected with their understandings of the world. For Nicola it was later still. None of the teachers I spoke with discussed examining these values during their initial teacher education and they appeared to develop these value positions independently of any formal education training.

The findings of this research should lead us to question whether we should be paying more attention to subject values during initial teacher education. Anecdotal accounts of the interviewing process for ITE courses outline how pre-service teachers can struggle with basic questions of why they want to teach their subject (Rawding 2010). Indeed, the trend in teacher education in England (England is rather a special case here and lies in contrast to teacher education trends in Ireland, Canada and Australia) is for teachers to be trained on school-led programmes with increasingly limited access to subject specialists (for a detailed critique of the impact of these policies on the development of geography teachers see Tapsfield *et al.* 2015). As the report from Tapsfield *et al.* suggests, this raises concerns not just about the supply of teachers but also about the range of exposure they get beyond their school placements and to other professionals.

Similarly, the Carter Review on initial teacher education in England emphasized the importance of subject knowledge and subject specific pedagogy:

> Teachers who understand the way pupils approach different subjects, understand the thinking behind pupils' methods and can identify common misconceptions are more likely to have a positive impact on pupil outcomes (Sadler and others, 2013 and Hill and others, 2005). We believe ITT should address subject-specific issues including phases of progression within the subject, links between subjects as well as common misconceptions and how to address these. This is important for both primary and secondary programmes. Both trainers and mentors should have a strong grasp of subject-specific pedagogy.
>
> *(Carter Review 2015: 58)*

The Review goes on to emphasize the importance of subject-specific pedagogy and makes particular mention of practical experiments in science and fieldwork in geography.

The trend, however, for both the recommendations made in the Carter Review and in teacher education generally is to focus on the technical aspects of teaching: the acquisition of teaching skills. The point being made here is a different one. I am not suggesting that skills are not an important part of teacher development; indeed, they are vital. However, trends in education change, and for teachers to adapt practice throughout their careers they will need to be able to rely on more than teaching skills, namely also an ability to assess, review and analyse education reform, in order to decide how to respond. Research into teachers' practices suggests that they do this anyway (see Ball and Goodson 1985; Ball and Bowe 1992; Ball 2003; Ball *et al.* 2012; and see Roberts 1995 for a geography example). However, no doubt teachers would be better equipped to adapt and respond to education reform if they had a better understanding of the value system they are bringing to the table.

To offer a specific example, in Chapter Six, I outlined how two teachers were responding to a similar educational reform environment, articulated differently in two schools. Both schools were enacting similar reform agendas and were using similar management strategies. The narratives from Mandy and Daisy suggest that how their schools were enacting these reforms varied. But what is more striking are the different ways that Mandy and Daisy responded to these changes. The data suggested that their responses to school reforms are not necessarily connected to the reform agendas that are taking place, but are possibly related to how the values that are implicit within them are communicated and the extent to which they are in line with the teacher's own values. I would suggest that making values an explicit part of the conversation in school and within initial teacher education programmes, could go some way to supporting teachers to understand and adapt to change that is taking place.

The argument has already been made that making values explicit is a key part of successful school reform. Fullan (2001) has outlined how making the moral purpose explicit is a key way to implement change successfully in schools. For teachers to be able to ride the ebb and flow of educational change, they will need an awareness of their own values, as well as an understanding of how value systems can change within educational contexts.

Related to the issue of teacher development is, of course, the issue of teacher recruitment and retention. Of the nine teachers who have featured in this book, one has retired and two have left teaching. Of the six that have remained in teaching, one has described herself as feeling miserable and two of the others talked about finding contexts they can work in where they feel comfortable. Disquiet is obvious even in such a small sample. The figures on teacher recruitment (four in ten teachers leaving the profession within their first year (*The Telegraph* 2015) suggest this is a wider trend. For this reason alone, it is important to pay attention to how teachers feel about their work.

However, the significance of the findings here goes beyond a sense of teacher happiness or wellbeing (although of course that is important). Being conscious of your values as a teacher is an important part of your teacher identity and how you relate to the contexts you work in.

Teacher professionalism

The last point that I wish to make here is to underline the professional part of the professional compass. For me, this is the most significant part of understanding why the professional compass matters. Metaphors have limitations and are, at best, a representation. The professional compass metaphor is valuable because it reflects the relationship between a teacher's sense of purpose and the professional knowledge landscape that can influence practice. A professional compass is individual and value-orientated.

The use of the term 'value' here is deliberate. Campbell (2003) distinguishes between morals and ethics, on the one hand, and values on the other. She highlights the interchangeability of ethics and morals as ideas but acknowledges that their usage differs. However, she distinguishes both from values, as these can be non-moral preferences held by individuals. For example, Steven's subject story, expressed through the idea of balance, represents a value for him, but one that would be difficult to justify as a moral or ethical code. Whilst the distinction between an individual's 'values' and professional 'ethics' is useful, the recognition of the importance of an individual's values is also, I would argue, part of their professionalism.

As Eraut (1994) notes, the values of the individual professional are only one set of values involved in ethical conduct at work. Schools, the educational community and legislative bodies (such as governments) also play a role in setting out the ethical landscape of teachers' practice. Lunt (2008) highlights how ethical codes, historically an important part of a profession's claims for public trust and self-regulation, are no longer sufficient. In the modern era of accountability, the status and role of the professions in society have changed. It is important then to note Eraut's (1994) four sets of values that can impinge on ethical conduct at work:

- Legal values
- Values of the profession
- Values of individual professionals
- Values of employing organizations.

This distinction draws attention to the mismatch between the values of the profession (in this case teaching), what regulatory frameworks require teachers to do by law (legal values), how schools interpret education policies and institute their own (values of employing organizations) and the individual values of the teacher. In the narratives explored in previous chapters, there are examples of when these values have come into conflict, and how teachers have sought to handle the situation. Daisy is an example of a teacher who has found such dilemmas difficult to reconcile and has decided to leave teaching as a result. Andrew has been able to reconcile these dilemmas more amicably, and Isobel has sought solace in her subject identity to help her find a sense of purpose in negotiating such challenges. These individual stories reflect what Lunt calls the 'modern ethical professionalism' which is determined by four ethical principles: competence, respect, integrity and responsibility. The narratives show how these principles have been differently interpreted by these teachers, and the different extent to which they have found reconciliation and resistance to be acts of integrity and responsibility. Viewed in this way, we can see echoes of the 'shifting moral landscapes' described by Clandinin and Hogan (1995).

However, discussions about ethics and morals (and to some extent values) are always tricky as they include expectations of how people should behave. In his work on professional ethics, Martin (2000) acknowledges that there is often a spiritual affiliation implied in discussions about ethics and morals. However, as Campbell (2003) notes, when discussing ethics and morals, it is important to consider the social and culture context from which particular values originate and whose values should take priority:

> In other words, in insisting that a good teacher is neither cruel nor unfair, we
> need not haggle over why this is essentially a moral imperative, rather than
> merely a culturally and socially constructed norm reflecting the interests of
> some over others.
>
> *(Campbell 2003: 15)*

The issue therefore is not to suggest that the individual values expressed here are 'right'
or 'wrong' or that the school values implicit in the policies or directives are 'right' or
'wrong', but to look at the dilemmas and contradictions that can occur when they
are misaligned.

The metaphor of a professional compass is useful here, as a compass points
towards the direction of magnetic north but the traveller need not follow this
pointer. The traveller may take an alternative and indirect route in order to reach
their destination. The compass does not show you how to get to your destination, but indicates where north is, so that you can orientate yourself within the
landscape, and consequently navigate direction. The compass therefore relies on
the traveller having both a map (and knowledge of the landscape), and an idea of
where they want to go. It is this last point, knowing where you want to go, that is
encompassed in Barton and Levstik's phrase 'a sense of purpose'.

The professional compass can therefore:

- Direct the teacher in their professional decision making (in this sense can
  be viewed as a part of their 'moral self', or moral compass) and, as such, can
  enable teachers to distinguish between teaching young people and seeking to
  educate them;
- Operate at a variety of levels within classroom practice and wider engagement
  in education and school life;
- Enable teachers to move beyond a 'delivery' mode of instruction to become
  'curriculum makers' responsible for a locally-relevant and responsive curriculum;
- Be seen as a powerful tool for individual reflection and meaning making,
  contributing to the teacher's professional identity, resilience and commitment.

There are clearly limitations to the professional compass metaphor. No doubt
there are some teachers who do not have a strong sense of their subject identity, or
who cannot recollect a strong subject story, and it is not the intention of this work
to suggest that they are somehow lacking or deficient. The aim of using the metaphor is to raise awareness of the subject dimension of teacher identity. The data
discussed suggest that awareness of this subject identity can be a powerful driver for
understanding teachers' work. Whilst the research upon which these observations
are based is limited in the number of teachers presented, the focus of the research
has been on developing a detailed understanding of their practice, shedding light
on the mechanisms that affect their work. The strength of the influence of subject
identity across a range of teachers with different backgrounds, histories and motivations, suggest that these findings are significant. The metaphor itself is merely a

convenient expression of the way that teachers have articulated this practice, and one that aligns neatly with the professional knowledge landscape metaphor.

It is also not the intention of this work to suggest that all teachers' values are going to be helpful or socially acceptable. In England, as in many other countries, professional values are a significant dimension of being granted Qualified Teacher Status and demonstrating professional values is an important part of gaining this status. Clearly, as in all professional contexts, there needs to be a frame of what is considered acceptable values and those that are deemed unprofessional need to be dealt with. However, the alternative is equally undesirable: that teachers are perceived as technical workers, unable to exercise professional judgement. The argument here is not that teachers should be given free rein to exercise their own values, but for a recognition that teachers' values, and particularly those related to their subject, are important and are deserving of more attention.

In the light of changes within education, we need a more nuanced way of understanding teachers' professional practice; delivery of subject content is an inadequate way of understanding teachers' work or their relationship with subject expertise. Having a professional compass can help teachers to deal with the range of demands placed on them through school-based reform. Awareness of a professional compass could enable teachers to see the positionality of these arguments and could be used by them to resist fads and trends and to focus on what is important in the educating of young people. The professional compass can be used as a way of understanding what it means to be a teacher in this day and age.

BIBLIOGRAPHY

Alexander, R. (2008) *Essays on pedagogy*. Abingdon: Routledge.

Al-Nofli, M. A. (2014) Omani students' definitions of geography. *International Research in Geographical and Environmental Education*. 23(2): 166–78.

Alsup, J. (2005) *Teacher identity discourses: negotiating personal and professional spaces*. New York: Routledge.

Apple, M. (1996) *Cultural politics and education*. Buckingham: Open University Press.

Askew, M., Brown, M., Rhodes, V., Wiliam, D. and Johnson, D. (1997) *Effective teachers of numeracy: report of a study carried out for the Teacher Training Agency*. London: King's College, University of London.

Aubrey C. (2007) *Leading and managing in the early years*. London: Sage.

Baldwin S. (2010) *Teachers' and students' 'relationships with knowledge': an exploration of the organisation of knowledge within disciplinary and educational contexts*. Unpublished PhD thesis: Lancaster University.

Bale, J. and McPartland, M. (1986) Johnstonian anarchy, inspectorial interest and the undergraduate education of PGCE geography students. *Journal of Geography in Higher Education*. 10(1): 61–70.

Ball, L. (1999) Back to the future: the development of educational policy in England. *Journal of Educational Administration*. 37(3): 200–28.

Ball, S. (2012) *Global education Inc.: new policy networks and the neo-liberal imaginary*. Abingdon: Routledge.

Ball, S. (2013) *Education, justice and democracy*. London: Class.

Ball, S. J. (1993) Education, Majorism and 'the Curriculum of the Dead'. *Journal of Curriculum Studies*. 1(2): 195–214.

Ball, S. J. (2003) The teacher's soul and the terrors of performativity. *Journal of Education Policy*. 18(2): 215–28.

Ball, S. J. and Bowe, R. (1992) Subject departments and the 'implementation' of national curriculum policy: an overview of the issues. *Journal of Curriculum Studies*. 24(2): 97–115.

Ball, S. J., Maguire, M. and Braun, A. (2012) *How schools do policy: policy enactments in secondary schools*. London: Routledge.

Ball, S. and Goodson, I. (eds) (1985) *Teachers' lives and careers*. London: Falmer Press.

Banks, F., Leach, J. and Moon, B. (1999) New understandings of teachers' pedagogic knowledge. In J. Leach and B. Moon (eds), *Learners and pedagogy*. London: Paul Chapman: 89–110.

Barber, M. (2007) *Instruction to deliver: fighting to transform Britain's public services*. London: Methuen.

Barnett, R. (2008) Changing modes of teacher professionalism: traditional, managerial, collaborative and democratic. In B. Cunningham (ed.), *Exploring professionalism*. London: Bedford Way Papers: 28–49.

Barratt-Hacking, E. (1996) Novice teachers and their geographical persuasions. *International Research in Geographical and Environmental Education*. 5(1): 77–86.

Barton, K. and Levstik, L. (2004) *Teaching history for the common good*. New Jersey: Lawrence Erlbaum.

Beauchamp, C. and Thomas, L. (2009) Understanding teacher identity: an overview of issues in the literature and implications for teacher education. *Cambridge Journal of Education*. 39(2): 175–89.

Becher, T. and Trowler, P. R. (2001) *Academic tribes and territories: intellectual enquiry and the culture of disciplines*. 2nd edition. Buckingham: The Society for Research into Higher Education and Open University Press.

Beijaard, D., Meijer, P. C. and Verloop, N. (2004) Reconsidering research on teachers' professional identity. *Teaching and Teacher Education*. 20(2): 107–28.

Bérci, M. E. (2006) The staircase of teacher development: a perspective on the process and consequences of the unity and integration of self. *Teacher Development*. 10(1): 55–71.

Bernstein, B. (1977) *Class, codes and control. Vol. 3: towards a theory of educational transmissions*. 2nd edition. London: Routledge and Kegan Paul.

Bernstein, B. (1990) *The structuring of pedagogic discourse*. London: Routledge.

Bernstein, B. (2000) *Pedagogy, symbolic, control and identity: theory, research, critique*. 2nd edition. Oxford: Rowman and Littlefield.

Biddulph, M. (2012) Young people's geographies and the school curriculum. *Geography*. 97(3): 155–62.

Biddulph, M. (2013) Where is the curriculum created? In D. Lambert and M. Jones, *Debates in geography education*. London: Routledge: 129–42.

Biddulph, M. (2014) Young people's geographies: implications for secondary school geography. In G. Butt (ed.), *Geography, education and the future*. London: Continuum: 44–57.

Biesta, G. (2009) Values and ideals in teachers' professional judgement. In S. Gerwirtz, P. Mahoney, I. Hextall and A. Cribb (eds), *Changing teacher professionalism: international trends, challenges and ways forward*. London: Routledge: 184–93.

Biesta, G. (2010) *Good education in an age of measurement: ethics, politics, democracy*. Boulder, CO: Paradigm.

Biesta, G. (2014) Pragmatising the curriculum: bringing knowledge back into the curriculum conversation, but via pragmatism. *The Curriculum Journal*. 25(1): 29–49.

Biesta, G. and Priestley, M. (2013) A curriculum for the twenty-first century? In M. Priestley and G. Biesta (eds), *Reinventing the curriculum: new trends in curriculum policy and practice*. London: Bloomsbury: 229–36.

Blankman, M., van der Schee, J., Volman, M. and Boogaard, M. (2015) Primary teacher educators' perception of desired and achieved pedagogical content knowledge in geography education in primary teacher training. *International Research in Geographical and Environmental Education*. 24(1): 80–94.

Bonnett, A. (2003) Geography as the world discipline: connecting popular and academic geographical imaginations. *Area*. 35(1): 55–63.

Bonnett, A. (2008) *What is geography?* London: Sage.

Bowe, R. and Ball, S. J. with Gold, A. (1992) *Reforming education and changing schools: case studies in policy sociology*. London: Routledge.

Britzman, D. P. (1986) Cultural myths in the making of a teacher: biography and social structure in teacher education. *Harvard Educational Review*. 56(4): 442–56.

Bronfenbrenner, U. (1979) *The ecology of human development: experiments by nature and design*. Cambridge, MA: Harvard University Press.

Brooks, C. (2006a) Geographical knowledge and teaching geography. *International Research in Geographical and Environmental Education*. 15(4): 353–69.

Brooks, C. (2006b) Geography teachers and making the school geography curriculum. *Geography*. 91(1): 75–83.

Bruner, J. (1986) *Actual minds, possible worlds*. Cambridge, MA: Harvard University Press.

Bruner, J. (1990) *Acts of meaning*. Cambridge, MA: Harvard University Press.

Bullough R. V. Jr (2011) Ethical and moral matters in teaching and teacher education. *Teaching and Teacher Education*. 27(1): 21–8.

Bullough, R. Jr and Draper, R. J. (2004) Mentoring and the emotions. *Journal of Education for Teaching: International Research and Pedagogy*. 30(3). 271–88, doi:10.1080/0260747042000309493.

Butt, G. (1997) *An investigation into the dynamics of the National Curriculum geography working group (1989–1990)*. Unpublished PhD thesis: University of Birmingham.

Calderhead, J. (1989) Reflective teaching and teacher education. *Teaching and Teacher Education*. 5(1): 43–51.

Calderhead, J. (1993) The contribution of research on teachers' thinking to the professional development of teachers. In C. Day, J. Calderhead and P. Denicolo (eds), *Research on teacher thinking*. London: Falmer Press: 11–18.

Calderhead, J. (1996) Teachers: beliefs and knowledge. In D. C. Berliner and R. C. Calfee (eds), *Handbook of educational psychology*. London: Prentice Hall International: 709–27.

Campbell, E. (2003) *The ethical teacher*. Maidenhead: Open University Press.

Campbell, R. J., Kyriakides, L., Muijs, R. D. and Robinson, W. (2004) Effective teaching and values: some implications for research and teacher appraisal. *Oxford Review of Education*, 30(4): 451–65, doi:10.1080/0305498042000303955.

Carlsen, W. S. (1999) Domains of teacher knowledge. In J. Gess-Newsome and N. G. Lederman (eds), *Examining pedagogical content knowledge*. Boston: Kluwer: 133–46.

Carr, D. (2006) Professional and personal values and virtues in education and teaching. *Oxford Review of Education*. (32)2: 171–83.

Carter, A. (2015) Carter Review of Initial Teacher Training (ITT). DFE Reference: DFE -00036-2015.

Castree, N. (2003) Environmental issues: relational ontologies and hybrid politics. *Progress in Human Geography*. 27(2): 203–11.

Catling, S. (2012) *Giving children voice: empowering pedagogy – a celebratory lecture marking the retirement of Professor Simon Catling*. Oxford: Oxford Brookes University.

Chalofsky, N. E. (2010) *Meaningful workplaces: reframing how and where we work*. San Francisco: Jossey-Bass.

Cheng Nga Yee, I. and Stimpson, P. G. (2004) *Conceptions of pedagogical content knowledge: a study of geography student teachers*. Paper presented at the Expanding Horizons in a Shrinking World Symposium, University of Strathclyde, Glasgow.

Christodoulou, D. (2014) *Seven myths about education*. London: Routledge.

Clandinin, D. J. and Connelly, F. M. (1995) *Teachers' professional knowledge landscapes*. New York: Teachers College, Columbia University.

Clandinin, D. J. and Hogan, P. (1995) Shifting moral landscapes: a story of Sonia's teacher education. In D. J. Clandinin and F. M. Connelly, *Teachers' professional knowledge landscapes*. New York: Teachers College, Columbia University.

Coe, R., Aloisi, C., Higgins, S. and Major L. E. (2014) *What makes great teaching? Review of the underpinning research*. The Sutton Trust: Durham University, Centre for Evaluation and Monitoring.

Connell, R. (2009) Good teachers on dangerous ground: towards a new view of teacher quality and professionalism. *Critical Studies in Education*. 50(3): 213–29.

Council of Europe (1985) Paper presented at the *Symposium on the Initial and In-Service Training of Teachers of Modern Languages*, Strasbourg.

Cresswell, T. (2004) *Place: a short introduction*. Chichester: Wiley-Blackwell.

Crites, S. (1971) The narrative quality of experience. *Journal of the American Academy of Religion*. 39(3): 291–311.

Cullingford, C. (1999) *An inspector calls: Ofsted and its effects on school standards*. London: Kogan Page.

Cunliffe, L. (2005) The problematic relationship between knowing how and knowing that in secondary art education. *Oxford Review of Education*. 31(4): 547–56.

Danielewicz, J. (1995) *Teaching selves: identity, pedagogy and teacher education*. Albany: State University of New York Press.

Daniels, P., Bradshaw, M., Shaw, D. and Sidaway, J. (eds) (2005) *An introduction to human geography: issues for the 21st Century*. 2nd edition. Harlow: Pearson Prentice Hall.

Day, C. (2004) *A passion for teaching*. London: RoutledgeFalmer.

Day, C. (2012) New lives of teachers. *Teacher Education Quarterly*. 39(1): 7–26.

Day, C. and Gu, Q. (2007) Variations in the conditions for teachers' professional learning and development: sustaining commitment and effectiveness over a career. *Oxford Review of Education*. 33(4): 423–43.

Day, C. and Gu, Q. (2010) *The new lives of teachers*. Abingdon: Routledge.

Day, C., Sammons, P., Stobart, G., Kington, A. and Gu, Q. (2007) *Teachers matter: connecting lives, work and effectiveness*. Maidenhead: Open University Press.

Deng, Z. (2007). Knowing the subject matter of a secondary-school science subject. *Journal of Curriculum Studies*, 39(5): 503–535, doi:10.1080/00220270701305362.

DfE (2010) *The importance of teaching*. Available online at https://www.gov.uk/government/uploads/system/uploads/attachment_data/file/175429/CM-7980.pdf (accessed 29 December 2015).

DfE (2012a) *Review of the National Curriculum in England: what can we learn from the English, mathematics and science curricula of high-performing jurisdictions?* Available online at https://www.gov.uk/government/uploads/system/uploads/attachment_data/file/184064/DFE-RR178.pdf (accessed 29 December 2015).

DfE (2012b) *Review of the National Curriculum in England: report on subject breadth in international jurisdictions*. Available online at https://www.gov.uk/government/uploads/system/uploads/attachment_data/file/197636/DFE-RR178a.pdf (accessed 29 December 2015).

Doecke, B. and Gill, M. (2000) Setting standards: confronting paradox. *English in Australia*. 9(1): 129–30.

Dunne, R. and Wragg, E. R. (1994) *Effective teaching*. London: Routledge.

Elbaz, F. (1990) Knowledge and discourse: the evolution of research on teacher thinking. In C. Day, M. Pope and P. Denicolo (eds), *Insights into teachers' thinking and practice*. Hampshire: Falmer: 15–42.

Elbaz, F. (1991) Research on teacher's knowledge: the evolution of a discourse. *Journal of Curriculum Studies*. (23)1: 1–19.

Ellis, V. (2007) Taking subject knowledge seriously: from professional knowledge recipes to complex conceptualizations of teacher development. *Curriculum Journal*. 18(4): 447–62.

Eraut, M. (1994) *Developing professional knowledge and competence*. London: Falmer Press.

Exley, B. E. (2008) Visual arts declarative knowledge: tensions in theory, resolutions in practice. *International Journal of Art and Design Education*. 27(3): 309–19.

Fang, Z. (1996) A review of research on teacher beliefs and practices. *Educational Research*. 38(1): 47–65.

Feiman-Nemser, S. and Floden, R. E. (2001) The cultures of teaching. In V. Richardson (ed.), *Handbook of research on teaching*, American Educational Research Association: 505–26.

Felbrich, A., Kaiser, G. and Schmotx C. (2014) The cultural dimension of beliefs: an investigation of future primary teachers' epistemological beliefs concerning the nature of mathematics in 15 countries. In S. Blömeke, H. Feng-Jui, G. Kaiser and W. H. Schmidt (eds), *International perspectives on teacher knowledge, beliefs and opportunities to learn*, Dordrecht: Springer: 209–30.

Fenstermacher, G. D. (1994) The knower and the known: the nature of knowledge in research on teaching. *Review of Research in Education*. 20(1): 3–56.

Firth, R. (2012) Disordering the coalition government's 'new' approach to curriculum design and knowledge: the matter of the discipline. *Geography*. 97(2): 86–94.

Foucault, M. (1979) *Discipline and punish: the birth of the prison*. London: Peregrine Books.

Frenzel, A. C., Goetz, T., Lüdtke, O., Pekrun, R. and Sutton, R. E. (2009) Emotional transmission in the classroom: exploring the relationship between teacher and student enjoyment. *Journal of Educational Psychology*. 101(3): 705–16.

Friedman, I. A. (2006) The bi-polar professional self of aspiring teachers: mission and power. *Teaching and Teacher Education*. 22(6): 722–39.

Fullan, M. (2001) *Leading in a culture of change*. San Francisco: Jossey-Bass.

Galen, J. A. (2010) Class, identity, and teacher education. *The Urban Review*. 42(4): 253–70.

Gallego, M. A. and Cole, M. (2001) Classroom cultures and cultures in the classroom. In V. Richardson (ed.), *Handbook of research on teaching*. American Educational Research Association: 951–97.

Galton, M. and MacBeath, J. (2008) *Teachers under pressure*. London: Sage and NUT.

Gess-Newsome, J. (1999) Pedagogical content knowledge: an introduction and orientation. In J. Gess-Newsome and N. G. Lederman (eds), *Examining pedagogical content knowledge*. Boston: Kluwer: 3–17.

Gillborn, D. (1991) The micropolitics of educational reform (Sheffield, Qualitative and Quantitative Studies in Education, University of Sheffield).

Gilroy, P. (1987) *There ain't no black in the Union Jack: the cultural politics of race and nation*. London: Hutchinson.

Goleman, D. (1995) *Emotional intelligence*. New York: Bantam Books.

Goodenough, W. H. (1994) Toward a working theory of culture. In R. Borotsky (ed.), *Assessing cultural anthropology*. New York: McGraw-Hill: 262–73.

Goodson, I. (1987) *School subjects and curriculum change: studies in curriculum history*. 2nd edition. London: Falmer Press.

Goodson, I. (2000) Professional knowledge and the teacher's life and work. In C. Day, A. Fernandez, T. E. Hauge and J. Moller (eds), *The life and work of teachers*. London: Falmer Press: 13–25.

Goodson, I. (2003) *Professional knowledge, professional lives: studies in education and change*. Maidenhead: Open University Press.

Goodson, I. and Hargreaves, A. (eds) (1996) *Teachers' professional lives*. London: Falmer Press.

Goodson, I. and Medway, P. (1990) Bringing English to order. Introduction in I. Goodson and P. Medway (eds), *Bringing English to order: the history and politics of a school subject*. London: Falmer Press: 1–46.

Goodson, I. and Sikes, P. (2001) *Life history research in educational settings: learning from lives*. Buckingham: Open University Press.

Goodson, I., Tedder, M., Gert J. J. Biesta, G. J. J. and Adair, N. (2011) *Narrative learning*. London: Routledge.

Graves, N. (2001) *School textbook research: the case of geography 1800–2000*. London: Institute of Education.

Gregory, D. (1994) *Geographical imaginations*. Oxford: Blackwell.

Grigutsch, S., Raatz, U. and Törner, G. (1998) Einstellungen gegenüber Mathematik bei Matheiklehrern. *Journal für Mathematik-Didaktik*. 19: 3–45, cited in Felbrich, A., Kaiser, G. and Schmotz, C. (2014) The cultural dimension of beliefs: an investigation of future primary teachers' epistemological beliefs concerning the nature of mathematics in 15 countries. In S. Blömeke, H. Feng-Jui, G. Kaiser and W. H. Schmidt (eds), *International perspectives on teacher knowledge, beliefs and opportunities to learn*. Dordrecht: Springer.

Grossman, P. L. (1990) *The making of a teacher: teacher knowledge and teacher education*. Columbia University: Teachers College Press.

Grossman, P. L. (1991) What are we talking about anyway? Subject matter knowledge of secondary English teachers. In J. Broby (ed.), *Advances in research on teaching* Vol. 2. Greenwich, CT: JAI Press Inc: 245–64.

Grossman, P. L., Wilson, S. M. and Shulman, L. (1989) Teachers of substance: subject matter knowledge for teaching. In M. C. Reynolds (ed.), *Knowledge base for the beginning teacher*. Oxford: Pergamon Press: 23–36.

Gudmundsdottir, S. (1990) Values in pedagogical content knowledge. *Journal of Teacher Education*. 41(3): 44–52.

Gudmundsdottir, S. (1991a) Pedagogical models of subject matter. In J. Brophy (ed.), *Advances in research on teaching*, Vol. 2. London: JAI Press: 265–304.

Gudmundsdottir, S. (1991b) Ways of seeing are ways of knowing: the pedagogical content knowledge of an expert English teacher. *Journal of Curriculum Studies*. 23(5): 409–21.

Hall, S. (1997) The work of representation. In S. Hall (ed.), *Representation: cultural representations and signifying practices*. Milton Keynes: Open University Press: 15–64.

Halse, C., Kennedy, K. and Cogan, J. J. (2004) The future direction of schooling. *International Journal of Educational Research*. 41(7–8): 584–94.

Hargreaves, A. (1991) Contrived congeniality: the micropolitics of teacher collaboration. In J. Blase (ed.), *The politics of life in schools: power, conflict and co-operation*. California: Sage: 46–72.

Hargreaves, A. (1994) *Changing teachers, changing times: teachers' work and culture in the postmodern age*. London: Cassell.

Hargreaves, A. (2001) Emotional geographies of teaching. *Teachers College Record*. 103(6): 1056–80.

Hargreaves, A. and Fullan, M. (2012) *Professional capital: transforming teaching in every school*. New York: Teachers College Press.

Hargreaves, A. and Shirley, D. (2009) The persistence of presentism. *Teachers College Record*. 111(11): 2505–34.

Hargreaves, D. (1995) School culture, school effectiveness and school improvement. *School Effectiveness and School Improvement*. 6(1): 23–46.

Hatch, T. (2013) Beneath the surface of accountability: answerability, responsibility and capacity-building in recent education reforms in Norway. *Journal of Educational Change*. 14(2): 113–38.

Hattie, J. (2008) *Visible learning: a synthesis of meta-analyses relating to achievement*. London: Routledge.

Heilbronn, R. and Yandell, J. (eds) (2010) *Critical practice in teacher education: a study of professional learning*. London: Institute of Education.

Helsby, G. (2000) Multiple truths and contested realities: the changing face of teacher professionalism in England. In C. Day, A. Fernandez, T. E. Hauge and J. Moller (eds), *The life and work of teachers*. London: Falmer Press: 93–108.

Helsby, G. and McCulloch, G. (eds) (1997) *Teachers and the National Curriculum*. London: Cassell.

Hill, H. C., Rowan, B. and Ball, D. L. (2005) Effects of teachers' mathematical knowledge for teaching on student achievement. *American Educational Research Journal*. 42(2): 371–406.

Hillocks, G. J. (1999) *Ways of thinking, ways of teaching*. New York: Teachers College.

Hirsch, E. D. (1987) *Cultural literacy: what every American needs to know*. Boston: Houghton Mifflin.

Holloway, S. L., Rice, S. P. and Valentine, G. (2003) *Key concepts in geography*: London: Sage.

Hubbard, P., Kitchin, R., Bartley, B. and Fuller, D. (2002) *Thinking geographically: space, theory and contemporary human geography*. London: Continuum.

Huddy, L. (2001) From social to political identity: a critical examination of social identity theory. *Political Psychology*. 22(1): 127–56.

Hunt, T. (2014) Lessons in Education from Singapore. Available at http://www.tristramhunt. com/lessons_in_education_from_singapore (accessed 4 January 2016).

Husbands, C. (1996) *What is history teaching? Language, ideas and meaning in learning about the past*. Buckingham: Open University Press.

Husbands, C. (2011) What do history teachers (need to) know? In I. Davies (ed.), *Debates in history teaching*. London: Routledge: 84–95.

Husbands, C., Kitson, A. and Pendry, A. (2003) *Understanding history teaching: teaching and learning about the past in secondary schools*. Maidenhead: Open University Press.

Isaacs, T. (2014) Curriculum and assessment reform gone wrong: the perfect storm of GCSE English. *The Curriculum Journal*. 25(1): 130–47.

Iwaskow, L. (2013) Geography: a fragile environment? *Teaching Geography*. 38(2): 53–5.

Jackson, P. (1989) *Maps of meaning*. London: Routledge.

Jackson, P. (1993) Changing ourselves: a geography of position. In R. J. Johnston (ed.), *The challenge for geography*. Oxford: Blackwell: 198–214.

Jackson, P. (2006) Thinking geographically. *Geography*. 91(3): 199–204.

Jalongo, M. R., Isenberg, J. P. and Gloria, G. (1995) *Teachers' stories: from personal narrative to professional insight*. San Francisco: Jossey-Bass Publishers.

Jewitt, L. (1998) *Personal experiences, values and the teaching of geography*. Unpublished MA dissertation, Institute of Education, London.

Johnston, R. J. (1991) *Geography and geographers: Anglo-American human geography since 1945*. 4th edition. London: Edward Arnold.

Johnston, R. J. (1993) *The challenge for geography*. Oxford: Blackwell.

Johnston, R. J. (2009) On geography, Geography and geographical magazines. *Geography*. 94(3): 207–14.

Kaniuka, T. S. (2012) Toward an understanding of how teachers change during school reform: considerations for educational leadership and school improvement. *Journal of Educational Change*. 13(3): 327–46.

Kinder, A. (2011) The National Curriculum review: what geography should we teach? *Teaching Geography*. 36(3): 93–5.

Korthagen, F. A. J. (2004) In search of the essence of a good teacher: towards a more holistic approach in teacher education. *Teaching and Teacher Education*. 20(1): 77–97.

Kroeber, A. L. and Kluckhohn, C. (1963) *Culture: a critical review of concepts and definitions*. New York: Vintage Books.

Kyriacou, C. (1997) *Effective teaching in schools: theory and practice*. 2nd edition. London: Stanley Thornes.

Lambert, D. (2002) Teaching through a lens: the role of subject expertise in teaching geography. In Y. C. Cheng, K. T. Tsui, K. W. Chow and M. M. C. Mok (eds), *Subject teaching and teacher education in the new century: research and innovation*. Hong Kong: The Hong Kong Institute of Education, Kluwer Academic Publishers: 349–74.

Lambert, D. (2003) Geography: a burden on the memory or a light in the mind? *Geography*. 88(1): 47.

Lambert, D. (2004) Geography. In J. White (ed.), *Rethinking the school curriculum*. Abingdon: RoutledgeFalmer: 75–86.

Lambert, D. (2013) Collecting our thoughts: school geography in retrospect and prospect. *Geography*. 98(1): 10–17.

Lambert, D. and Morgan, J. (2010) *Teaching geography 11–18: a conceptual approach*. Maidenhead: Open University Press.

Lane, R. (2015) Experienced geography teachers' PCK of students' ideas and beliefs about learning and teaching. *International Research in Geographical and Environmental Education*. 24(1): 43–57.

Lasky, S. (2005) A sociocultural approach to understanding teacher identity, agency and professional vulnerability in a context of secondary school reform. *Teaching and Teacher Education*. 21(8): 899–916.

Lawton, D. (1989) *Education, culture and the National Curriculum*. London: Hodder and Stoughton.

Leat, D., Thomas, U. and Reid, A., (2012) The epistemological fog in realising learning to learn in European curriculum policies. *European Educational Research Journal*. 11(3): 400–412.

Lee, A. (1996) *Gender, literacy, curriculum: re-writing school geography*. Abingdon: Taylor and Francis.

Levinson, R. (2007) *Towards a pedagogical framework for the teaching of controversial socio-scientific issues to secondary school students in the age range 14–19*. Unpublished PhD thesis. London: Institute of Education.

Lips-Wiersma, M. and Morris, L. (2011) *The map of meaning: a guide to sustaining our humanity in the world of work*. Sheffield: Greenleaf.

Livingstone, D. (1993) *The geographical tradition*. Oxford: Blackwell.

Lortie, D. (1975) *Schoolteacher*. Chicago: University of Chicago Press.

Lunt I. (2008) Ethical issues in professional life. In B. Cunningham (ed.), *Exploring professionalism*. London: Bedford Way Papers, IOE Press: 73–98.

MacLure, M. (1993) Arguing for your self: identity as an organising principle in teachers' jobs and lives. *British Educational Research Journal*. 19(4): 311–22.

McBer, H. (2000) *Research into Teacher Effectiveness*. London: Report to the DfEE.

McCulloch, G., Gill, H. and Knight, P. (2000) *The politics of professionalism: teachers and the curriculum*. London: Continuum.

Maguire, M., Perryman, J., Ball, S. and Braun, A. (2011) The ordinary school: what is it? *British Journal of Sociology of Education*. 32(1): 1–16.

Marsden, W. E. (1997) On taking the geography out of geographical education. *Geography*, 82(3): 241–52.

Martin, F. (2005) Ethnogeography: a future for primary geography and primary geography research? *International Research in Geographical and Environmental Education*. 14(4): 364–71.

Martin, F. (2006) Knowledge bases for effective teaching: beginning teachers' development as teachers of primary geography. In D. Schmeink (ed.), *Research on learning and teaching in primary geography*. Karlsruhe: Pädagogische Hochschule Karlsruhe: 149–84.

Martin, M. W. (2000) *Meaningful work: rethinking professional ethics*. Oxford. Oxford University Press.

Maton, K. (2014) *Knowledge and knowers: towards a realist sociology of education*. London: Routledge.

Matthews, J. A. and Herbert, D. T. (eds) (2004) *Unifying geography: common heritage, shared future*. Abingdon: Routledge.

Meijer, P. C., Korthagen, F. A. J. and Vasalos, A. (2009) Supporting presence in teacher education: the connection between the personal and professional aspects of teaching. *Teaching and Teacher Education*, 25(2): 297–308, doi:10.1016/j.tate.2008.09.013.

Meyer, J. H. F. and Land, R. (2005) Threshold concepts and troublesome knowledge (2): epistemological considerations and a conceptual framework for teaching and learning. *Higher Education*. 49(3): 373–88.

Mitchell, D. and Lambert, D. (2015) Subject knowledge and teacher preparation in English secondary schools: the case of geography. *Teacher Development*. 19(3): 365–80.

Monk, D. H. (1994) Subject matter preparation of secondary mathematics and science teachers and student achievement. *Economics of Education Review*. 13(2): 125–45.

Moore, A., Edwards, G., Halpin, D. and George, R. (2002) Compliance, resistance and pragmatism: the reconstruction of schoolteacher identities in a period of intensive educational reform. *British Educational Research Journal*. 28(4): 551–65.

Morgan, A. (2011) Morality and geography education. In G. Butt (ed.), *Geography, education and the future*. London: Continuum: 187–208.

Morgan, J. (2010) After the crash . . . place, space and identity. In G. Butt (ed.), *Geography, education and the future*. London: Continuum: 109–22.

Morgan, J. (2011) Knowledge and the school geography curriculum: a rough guide for teachers. *Teaching Geography*. 36(3): 90–92.

Morgan, J. and Lambert, D. (2005) *Geography: teaching school subjects 11–19*. London: Routledge.

Mortimore, P., Sammons, P., Stoll, L., Lewis, D. and Ecob, R. (1988) *School matters*. Wells: Open Books.

Muijs, R. D. and Reynolds, D. (2003) Student background and teacher effects on achievement and attainment in mathematics. *Educational Research and Evaluation*. 9(1): 289–313.

Muijs, R. D. and Reynolds, D. (2011) *Effective teaching: evidence and practice*. London: Sage.

Nias, J. (1987) *Seeing anew: teachers' theories of action*. Deelong: Deakin University.

Nias, J. (1989) *Primary teachers talking: a study of teaching as work*. London: Routledge.

Nias, J. (1991) Changing times, changing identities: grieving for a lost self. In R. G. Burgess (ed.), *Educational research and evaluation*. London: Falmer Press: 139–56.

OECD (2005) *Teachers matter: attracting, developing and retaining effective teachers*. Paris: Organisation for Economic Co-operation and Development (OECD).

Ofsted (2005) *Subject report: geography in primary school*. No. HMI 2344: TSO.

Paechter, C. F. (2000) *Changing school subjects: power, gender, and curriculum*. Buckingham: Open University Press.

Pajares, M. F. (1992) Teachers' beliefs and educational research: cleaning up a messy construct. *Review of Educational Research*. 62(3): 307–32.

Parker, D. C., Pushor, D. and Kitchen, J. (2011) Narrative inquiry in teaching and teacher education. *Advances in Research on Teaching*, 13: 3–68.

Peal, R. (2014) *Progressively worse: the burden of bad ideas in British schools*. London: Civitas.

Pedder, D., James, M. and MacBeath, J. (2005) How teachers value and practise professional learning. *Research Papers in Education*. 20(3): 209–43.

Perks, D. (2007) *What is science education for?* London: Institute for Ideas.

Perryman, J. (2006) Panoptic performativity and school inspection regimes: disciplinary mechanisms and life under special measures. *Journal of Education Policy*. 21(2): 147–61.

Pierce, C. (2013) *Education in the age of biocapitalism: optimising educational life for a flat world*. New York: Palgrave Macmillan.

Popkewitz, T. S. (ed.) (1987) *The formation of school subjects: the struggle for creating an American institution*. London: Falmer.

Power, S. (1996) *The pastoral and the academic: conflict and contradiction in the curriculum*. London: Cassell.

Prentice, R. (1997) Creating more contented teachers. In A. Hudson and D. M. Lambert (eds), *Exploring futures in initial teacher education*. London: Institute of Education: 411–26.

Preston, L. (2014) Australian primary in-service teachers' conceptions of geography. *International Research in Geographical and Environmental Education*. 24(2): 167–80.

Priestley, M., Robinson, S. and Biesta, G. J. J. (2012) Teacher agency, performativity and curriculum change: reinventing the teacher in the Scottish curriculum for excellence? In B. Jeffrey and G. Troman (eds), *Performativity across UK education: ethnographic cases of its effects, agency and reconstructions*. Painswick: E&E Publishing: 87–108.

Pring, R. (2013) *The life and death of secondary education for all*. London: Routledge.

Pring, R., Hayward, G., Hodgson, A., Johnson, J., Keep, E., Oancea, A., Rees, G., Spours, K. and Wilde, S. (2009) *Education for all: the future of education and training for 14–19 year olds*. London; Routledge.

Prosser, J. (ed.) (1999) *School Culture*. London: Paul Chapman.

Puttick, S. (2012) Geography teachers' conceptions of knowledge. *Teaching Geography*. 37(2): 73–5.

Ravitch, D. (2000) The educational backgrounds of history teachers. In P. N. Stearns, P. Seixas and S. Wineburg (eds), *Knowing, teaching, and learning history: national and international perspectives*. New York: New York University Press.

Rata, E. (2012) The politics of knowledge in education. *British Educational Research Journal*. 38(1): 103–24.

Rawding, C. (2010) What are the connections between subject developments in academic and school geography? *International Research in Geographical and Environmental Education*. 19(2): 119–25.

Rawling, E. (2001) *Changing the subject: the impact of national policy on school geography 1980–2000*. Sheffield: Geographical Association.

Reynolds, J. and Skilbeck, M. (1976) *Culture and the classroom*. London: Open Books.

Roberts, M. (1995) Interpretations of the geography national curriculum: a common curriculum for all? *Journal of Curriculum Studies*. 27(2): 187–205.

Roberts, M. (2010) Where's the geography? Reflections on being an external examiner. *Teaching Geography*. 35(3): 112–113.

Roberts M. (2014) Powerful knowledge and geographical education. *The Curriculum Journal*. 25(2): 187–209.

Rockoff, J. E., Jacob, B. A., Kane, T. J. and Staiger, D. O. (2011) Can you recognize an effective teacher when you recruit one? *Education*. 6(1): 43–74.

Ross E. W. and Gibson, R. (2007) *Neoliberalism and education reform*. Casskill, NJ: Hampton Press.

Rynne, E. and Lambert, D. (1997) The continuing mismatch between students' undergraduate experiences and the teaching demands of the geography classroom: experience of pre-service secondary geography teachers. *Journal of Geography in Higher Education*. 21(1): 187–98.

Sachs, J. (2003) *The activist teaching profession*. Buckingham: Open University Press.

Sadler, P. M., Sonnert, G., Coyle, H. P., Cook-Smith, N. and Miller, J. L. (2013) The influence of teachers' knowledge on student learning in middle school physical science classrooms. *American Educational Research Journal.* 50(5): 1020–49.

Sammons P., Day C., Kington A., Gu Q., Stobart G. and Smees, R. (2007) Exploring variations in teachers' work, lives and their effects on pupils: key findings and implications from a longitudinal mixed-method study. *British Educational Research Journal.* 33(5): 681–701.

Sarason, S. B. (1982) *The culture of the school and the problem of change.* 2nd edition. Boston: Allyn & Bacon.

Sayer, A. (2005) *The moral significance of class.* Cambridge: Cambridge University Press.

Sayer, A. (2011) *Why things matter to people: social science, values and ethical life.* Cambridge: Cambridge University Press.

Schön, D. A. (1987) *Educating the reflective practitioner.* San Francisco: Jossey-Bass.

Shulman, L. (1986) Those who understand: knowledge growth in teaching. *Educational Researcher.* 15(2): 4–14.

Shulman, L. (1987) Knowledge and teaching: foundation of the new reform. *Harvard Educational Review.* 57(1): 1–22.

Shurmer-Smith, P. (2002) The trouble with theory. In P. Shurmer-Smith (ed.), *Doing cultural geography.* London: Sage: 11–18.

Sikes, P., Measor, L. and Woods, P. (1985) *Teachers' careers: crises and continuities.* London: Falmer.

Sinnema, C. and Aitken, G. (2013) Trends in international curriculum development. In M. Priestley and G. J. J. Biesta (eds), *Reinventing the curriculum: new trends in curriculum policy and practice.* London: Bloomsbury: 141–64.

Slater, F. (1996) Values: towards mapping their locations in a geography education. In W. A. Kent, D. Lambert, M. Naish and F. A. Slater (eds), *Geography in education: viewpoints on teaching and learning.* Cambridge: Cambridge University Press: 201–30.

Smith, J. P. and Girod, M. (2003) John Dewey and psychologizing the subject-matter: big ideas, ambitious teaching, and teacher education. *Teaching and Teacher Education.* 19(3): 295–307.

Smith, R. G. (2007) Developing professional identities and knowledge: becoming primary teachers. *Teachers and Teaching.* 13(4): 377–97.

Søreide, G. E. (2006) Narrative construction of teacher identity: positioning and negotiation. *Teachers and Teaching: Theory and Practice.* 12(5): 527–47.

Standish, A. (2009) *Global perspectives in the geography curriculum: reviewing the moral case for geography.* Oxford: Routledge.

Starratt, R. J. (1994) *Building an ethical school: a practical response to the moral crisis in schools.* London: Falmer.

Stengel, B. S. (1997) "Academic discipline" and "school subject": contestable curricular concepts. *Journal of Curriculum Studies.* 29(5): 585–602.

Sternhagen, K., Reich, G. A. and Muth, W. (2013) Disciplined judgment: toward a reasonably constrained constructivism. *Journal of Curriculum and Pedagogy.* 10(1): 55–72.

Stoddart, D. R. (1987) To claim the high ground: geography for the end of the century. *Transactions of the Institute of British Geographers.* 12(3): 327–36.

Stoll, L. (1998) *School culture.* London: School Improvement Network.

Stoll, L. (1999) School culture: black hole or fertile garden for school improvement. In J. Prosser (ed.), *School culture.* London: Paul Chapman: 30–47.

Sutton, R. E. and Wheatley, K. F. (2003) Teachers' emotions and teaching: a review of the literature and directions for future research. *Educational Psychology Review.* 15(4): 327–58.

Tapsfield, A. with Roberts, M. and Kinder, A. (2015) *Geography initial teacher education and teacher supply in England: a national research report by the Geographical Association.* Sheffield: Geographical Association.

The Telegraph (2015) Four-in-10 new teachers quit within a year union warns, 31 Mar. Available online at http://www.telegraph.co.uk/education/educationnews/11505837/ Four-in-10-new-teachers-quit-within-a-year-union-warns.html (accessed 29 December 2015).

Thrift, N. (2002) The future of geography. *Geoforum.* 33: 291–98.

Thrift, N. and Walling, D. (2000) Geography in the United Kingdom 1996–2000. *The Geographical Journal.* 166(2): 1–29.

Thomas, E. (2000) *Culture and schooling: building bridges between research, praxis and professionalism.* Chichester: John Wiley & Sons.

Thompson, M. (1995) *Professional ethics and the teacher: an educated talent in the service of society.* Retrieved from Monograph for the Directors of the General Teaching Council.

Timperley, H., Wilson, A., Barrar, H. and Fung, I. (2007) *Teacher professional learning and development: best evidence synthesis iteration.* Wellington, New Zealand: Ministry of Education. Available online at http://www.educationcounts.govt.nz/publications/ series/2515/15341 (accessed 29 December 2015).

Trent, J. and Lim, J. (2010) Teacher identity construction in school–university partnerships: discourse and practice. *Teaching and Teacher Education.* 26(8): 1609–18.

Tryggvason, M. T. (2009) Why is Finnish teacher education successful? Some goals Finnish teacher educators have for their teaching. *European Journal of Teacher Education.* 32(4): 369–82.

Turner-Bisset, R. (2001) *Expert teaching: knowledge and pedagogy to lead the profession.* London: Fulton.

Turvey, A. (2005) Who'd be an English teacher? *Changing English.* 12(1): 3–18.

Twiselton, S. and Webb, D. (1998) The trouble with English: the challenge of developing subject knowledge in school. In C. Richards, N. Simco and S. Twiselton (eds), *Primary teacher education high status? High standards?* London: Falmer Press: 150–64.

Tyack, D. and Cuban, L. (1995) *Tinkering toward utopia: a century of public school reform.* Cambridge, MA: Harvard University Press.

Unwin, T. (1992) *The place of geography.* Harlow: Longman Scientific and Technical.

Van Mannen, M. (1995) On the epistemology of reflective practice. *Teachers and Teaching: Theory and Practice.* 1: 33–49.

van Veen, K. and Lasky, S. (2005) Emotions as a lens to explore teacher identity and change: different theoretical approaches. *Teaching and Teacher Education.* 21(8): 895–8, doi:10.1016/j.tate.2005.06.002.

Walford, R. (1996) 'What is geography?' An analysis of definitions provided by prospective teachers of the subject. *International Research in Geographical and Environmental Education.* 5(1): 69–76.

Walford, R. (2001) *Geography in British schools 1850–2000.* London: Woburn Press.

Weber, S. and Mitchell, C. (1996) Drawing ourselves into teaching: studying the images that shape and distort teacher education. *Teaching and Teacher Education.* 12(3): 303–13.

Wertsch, J. V. (2000) Is it possible to teach beliefs, as well as knowledge about history? In P. N. Stearns, P. Seixas and S. Wineburg (eds), *Knowing, teaching, and learning history: national and international perspectives.* New York: New York University Press: 38–50.

Wheelahan, L. (2010) *Why knowledge matters in curriculum: a social realist argument.* London: Routledge.

White, J. (2004) Introduction. In J. White (ed.), *Rethinking the school curriculum.* Abingdon: RoutledgeFalmer: 1–20.

White, K. R. (2009) Connecting religion and teacher identity: the unexplored relationship between teachers and religion in public schools. *Teaching and Teacher Education.* 25(6): 857–66.

Whitty, G. (1989) The New Right and the national curriculum: state control or market forces? *Journal of Education Policy.* 4(4): 329–41.

Whitty, G. (2008) Changing modes of teacher professionalism. In B. Cunningham (ed.), *Exploring professionalism.* London: Institute of Education, University of London: 28–49.

Williams, R. (1981) *Culture.* London: Fontana.

Wu, Z. (2004) Being, understanding and naming: teachers' life and work in harmony. *International Journal of Educational Research.* 41 (4): 307–23.

Yandell, J. (2013) *The social construction of meaning: reading literature in urban English classrooms.* New York: Routledge.

Youdell, D. (2011) *School trouble: identity, power and politics in education.* Abingdon: Routledge.

Young, M. (2008) *Bringing knowledge back in: from social constructivism to social realism in the sociology of education.* London: Routledge.

Young. M. (2011a) The return to subjects: a sociological perspective on the UK coalition government's approach to the 14–19 curriculum. *The Curriculum Journal.* 22(2): 265–78.

Young. M. (2011b) Discussion to part 3 (mediating forms of geographical knowledge). In Butt, G. (ed.), *Geography education and the future.* London: Continuum: 181–3.

Zeichner, K. M. and Liston, D. P. (1987) Teaching student teachers to reflect. *Harvard Educational Review.* 57(1): 23–49.

Zembylas, M. (2003) Interrogating teacher identity: emotion, resistance, and self-formation. *Educational Theory.* 53(1): 107–27.

Zembylas, M. (2010) Emotions and teacher identity: a poststructural perspective. *Teachers and Teaching.* 9(3): 37–41.

INDEX